In Praise of Literature

In Praise of Literature

Zygmunt Bauman and
Riccardo Mazzeo

polity

The right of Zygmunt Bauman, Riccardo Mazzeo to be identified as Authors of this Work has been asserted in accordance with the UK Copyright, Designs and Patents Act 1988.

First published in 2016 by Polity Press

Polity Press
65 Bridge Street
Cambridge CB2 1UR, UK

Polity Press
350 Main Street
Malden, MA 02148, USA

ISBN-13: 978-1-5095-0268-4
ISBN-13: 978-1-5095-0269-1(pb)

A catalogue record for this book is available from the British Library.
Names: Bauman, Zygmunt, 1925- author. | Mazzeo, Riccardo.
Title: In praise of literature / Zygmunt Bauman, Riccardo Mazzeo.
Description: Cambridge, U.K. ; Malden, MA : Polity, 2015. | Includes
    bibliographical references and index.
Identifiers: LCCN 2015025860| ISBN 9781509502684 (hardback) | ISBN
    9781509502691 (paperback)
Subjects: LCSH: Literature and society. | Literature--History and
    criticism--Theory, etc. | BISAC: LITERARY CRITICISM / Semiotics & Theory.
Classification: LCC PN51 B325 2016 | DDC 809/.933552--dc23 LC record
available at http://lccn.loc.gov/2015025860

Typeset in 11 on 14 pt Sabon by
Servis Filmsetting Ltd, Stockport, Cheshire
Printed and bound in Great Britain by Clays Ltd, St. Ives PLC

For further information on Polity, visit our website:
politybooks.com

Contents

The phrase, the world wants to be deceived, has become truer than had ever been intended. People are not only, as the saying goes, falling for the swindle; if it guarantees them even the most fleeting gratification they desire a deception which is nonetheless transparent to them. They force their eyes shut and voice approval, in a kind of self-loathing, for what is meted out to them, knowing fully the purpose for which it is manufactured. Without admitting it they sense that their lives would be completely intolerable as soon as they no longer clung to satisfactions which are none at all.

Theodor W. Adorno, 'Culture Industry Reconsidered',
trans. Anson G. Rabinbach, in *The Culture Industry*,
Routledge 1991, p.89

The official practise of humanism is completed by accusing everything truly human and in no way official of inhumanity. For criticism takes from man his meagre spiritual possessions, removing the veil which he himself looks upon as benevolent. The anger aroused in him by the unveiled image is diverted to those who tear the veil, in keeping with the hypothesis of Helvetius that truth never damages anyone except him who utters it.

Theodor W. Adorno, 'Culture and Administration', trans.
Wes Blomster, *Telos* 37, 1978, p. 106

The simple fact must be recognized that that which is specifically cultural is that which is removed from the naked necessity of life. [...] Culture – that which goes beyond the system of self-preservation of the species. [...] The sacrosanct irrationality of culture.

Ibid., p. 94, 100, 97

(M)aterial reality is called the world of exchange value [whereas culture] refuses to accept the domination of that world.

Theodor W. Adorno, *Minima Moralia*, trans.
E. F. N. Jephcott, Verso 1974, p. 44

Preface

The subject-matter of our conversation-in-letters, reproduced below, is the notoriously (and according to
some people 'essentially') contested issue: the relation
between literature (and arts in general) and sociology
(or, more generally, a branch of the humanities that
claim a scientific status).

Both literature, together with the rest of the arts, and
sociology are part and parcel of culture; the above-quoted
Theodor W. Adorno's statements and assessments of the
nature and role of culture – as 'going beyond the system
of self-preservation' by 'tearing the veil' that culture's
prospective beneficiaries may self-deceive into looking
upon as benevolent – apply to both in equal measure.
All the same, it is our view that literature and sociology
are linked to each other more intimately and cooperate
with each other more closely than is common among the
various types of cultural products, and certainly much
more than their administratively motivated and imposed
separation would suggest.

We attempt to argue and to demonstrate that literature

and sociology share the field they explore, their subject-matter and topics – as well as (at least to a substantive degree) their vocation and social impact. As one of us said, in trying to spell out the nature of their kinship and cooperation, literature and sociology are 'complementary, supplementary to each other and reciprocally enriching. They are by no means in competition [. . .] – let alone at loggerheads or cross-purposes. Knowingly or not, deliberately or matter-of-factly, they pursue the same purpose; one could say "they belong to the same business".'[1] This is why, if you are a sociologist trying to crack the mystery of the human condition and so to tear the veil woven of pre-judgements and insinuated or self-concocted misconceptions, 'if you are after the "real life" rather than "truth" overloaded with the doubtful and presumptuous "knowledge" of *homunculi* born and bred in test-tubes, then you can hardly choose better than to take a hint from the likes of Franz Kafka, Robert Musil, Georges Perec, Milan Kundera or Michel Houllebecq'. Literature and sociology feed each other. They also cooperate in drawing each other's cognitive horizons and help to correct each other's occasional blunders.

What we had in mind, however, when conducting our exchange was neither to compose another reconstruction of the long chronicle of changing scholarly views on the multi-faceted relationship between arts and human/social sciences, nor to take a snapshot of its present stage. Conducted and recorded from the perspective of mainly sociological interests and concerns, our conversations are not an exercise in the theory of literature – let alone a reconstruction of its long and rich history. We've tried instead to present that relation in action: to trace, note and document the shared aspirations, mutual inspirations and interchange of these two kinds of inquiry into the human condition – human ways of being-in-the-world complete with their joys and sorrows, deployed as well as neglected or wasted human potentials, prospects and hopes, expectations and frustrations. Both literature and sociology do all that (at least attempt to do it and most surely are called to go on attempting) – while deploying distinct, albeit mutually complementary, strategies, tools and methods.

Classifying and filing literature among the arts, while sociology struggles earnestly – though with mixed success – for being classified and filed among the sciences, cannot but leave a deep imprint on common views of their mutual relationship – as well as on the priorities of their practitioners. For that reason, drawing boundaries has been attracting more attention on both sides of the assumed division than building bridges and facilitating cross-border traffic (bringing to both sides as the result, in our view, incomparably more harm than profit), while the job of checking obligatory identity cards commanded on the whole incomparably more attention and dedication than issuing (few and far between) travel documents – as if to confirm Frederick Barth's observation that, rather than borders being drawn because of the presence of differences, differences are avidly sought and invented because borders have been drawn.[2] Each of the two juxtaposed classes of cultural products sets stern demands for all applicants for inclusion; rigorous, stringent and onerous prescriptions and proscriptions are codified in order to guard the unique identity and territorial sovereignty of each entity. On the scale of conformity to the rules, the crossbars tend to be set discouragingly high to keep away insufficiently disciplined

---

applicants who threaten to wash away the class privilege together with borderline stockades.

Differences in 'methods' of proceeding, just like the points at which literatures and social-scientific research feel allowed to announce arrival at their respective destinations, are indeed multiple and variegated.[3] Two of the differences, however, are, as far as we are concerned, central to the distinction between the two ways of investigating the human condition – while, simultaneously, to their complementarity. This duality was splendidly caught by Georgy Lukács already in his 1914 study: 'Art always says "And yet!" to life. The creation of forms is the most profound confirmation of the existence of a dissonance [. . .] [T]he novel, in contrast to other genres whose existence resides within the finished form, appears as something in process of becoming'.[4] Let's add that a great part of – perhaps most – sociological study belongs to the family of those 'other genres': it aims towards completeness, conclusiveness and closure. Committed to this task, it is willing to skip, relegate to the margin, or efface from the picture as irrelevant idiosyncratic anomaly, everything uniquely personal – subjective – as quirky, offbeat and aberrant. It strives to unravel the uniform and general while eliminating the peculiar and distinct as quaint and anomalous. As Lukács insists, however, it could not be otherwise than 'that the outward form of the novel' is 'essentially biographical'. He warns right away that 'the fluctuation between a conceptual system which can never completely capture life and a life complex which can never attain completeness is immanently utopian'.

And so we confront on the one hand the organically heteronomic and endemically dissonant social setting of individual life, and on the other the earnest if doomed effort of the individual to conjure up a cohesive totality out of fragmented life, and a steadfast trajectory out of a series of biographic twists and swivels weather-cock-style. The first induces the fallacy of imputing logic and rationality to an illogical and irrational condition; the other incites the error of spying a self-propelled and self-guided exploit in a tangle of disparate and inconsistent pulls and pushes. One danger is endemic to sociological undertakings; the other to novel-writing. Neither sociology, nor literature, can conquer their respective menaces on their own. They can, however, circumvent or vanquish both, if – and only if – they join forces. And it is precisely their *difference* that gives them the chance of victory under the sign of *complementarity*. To quote Milan Kundera's – as concise as it is cogent – way of putting it: 'the founder of the modern era is not only Descartes but also Cervantes [. . .] If it is true that philosophy and science have forgotten about man's being, it emerges all the more plainly that with Cervantes a great European art took shape that is nothing other than the investigation of this forgotten being.'[5] And to quote also his wholehearted endorsement of Hermann Broch's assertion that 'the sole raison d'être of a novel is to discover what only a novel can discover'. We would add: without that discovery, sociology would risk becoming a one-legged walker.

We believe that the relationship in question bears all the marks of a 'sibling rivalry': a mixture of cooperation and competition, only to be expected among beings who are bound to engage in the pursuit of similar objectives while being judged, evaluated and recognized or denied recognition on the ground of distinct, though comparable, types of results. Novels and sociological studies arise from the same curiosity and have similar cognitive purposes; sharing parenthood and bearing indisputable, palpable family resemblance, they watch each other's advances with a blend of admiration and comradely jealousy. Novel-writers and the writers of sociological texts in the last account explore the same ground: the vast human experience of being-in-the-world that (to quote José Saramago) 'bear[s] witness to the passage through this world of men and women who for good or bad reasons have not only lived but also left a mark, a presence, an influence, which, having survived to this day, will continue to affect generations to come'.[6] Novel-writers and the writers of sociological texts dwell in the shared household: in what the Germans call *die Lebenswelt*, the 'lived world', the world perceived and recycled by its residents (its 'auctors' – that is, simultaneously its actors and authors) into the wisdom of 'common sense', re-moulded into the art of life reflected in their life practices. Knowingly or not, purposefully or just matter-of-factly, they are both engaged in a sort of 'secondary (or derivative) hermeneutics': a continuous reinterpretation of entities that are outcomes of preceding interpretations – realities formed by interpretative exertions of the *hoi polloi* and stored in their *doxa* (common sense: ideas one thinks with, but little – if at all – about).

On numerous past occasions, novel-writers (like other visionary artists) were first to note and scrutinize the incipient changes of track or new trends in the challenges that their contemporaries faced and struggled to tackle; novelists managed to spot and catch new departures at a stage in which, for most sociologists, they would remain unnoticed, or dismissed and unattended on account of their marginality and apparently irrevocable assignment to minority status. We are currently witnessing another such occasion. Once more in the history of modern times, novel-writers join film-makers and visual artists in the avant-garde of public reflection, debate and awareness. They are pioneering insight into the novel condition of men and women in our ever more deregulated, atomized, privatized society of consumers: people smarting under the tyranny of the moment, doomed to lead a hurried life and to join in the cult of novelty. They explore and portray transient joys and lasting depressions, fears, indignation, dissent and half- or whole-hearted inchoate attempts at resistance – ending in partial victories or ostensible (though hopefully temporary) defeats. Awakened, inspired and boosted by them, sociology tries hard to recycle their insights into authoritative statements grounded in systematic *sine ira et studio* ('with neither hate nor zeal') research. The career study of that process serves us as a key to unpacking the pattern of the relation and mutual interdependence between two, artistic and scientific, cultures – as well as to estimating the degree to which each of the two business associates owes its progress to the incentive, enlightenment, spur and animus received from the other.

To conclude the message which we conversationalists attempt to convey: novel-writers and the writers of sociological texts may explore this world from different perspectives, seeking and producing different types of 'data' – and yet their products bear unmistakable marks of shared origin. They feed each other, and depend on each other in their agenda, discoveries and the contents of their messages; they reveal the truth, the whole truth and nothing but the truth of the human condition only when staying in each other's company, remaining attentive to each other's findings, and engaged in a continuous dialogue. Only together can they rise up to the challenging task of untangling and laying bare the complex entwining of biography and history, as well as of individual and society: that totality we are daily shaping while being shaped by it.

Z. B. and R. M.

I
The Two Sisters

Riccardo Mazzeo You have clearly articulated the reasons why literature is so important for sociology, to the point of considering the two disciplines as 'sisters': both are indeed disposed to constantly shredding the veil of pre-interpretation[1] – as Milan Kundera puts it – as seen in the work *Don Quixote* by Cervantes.

To heed the complexity and the infinite variety of human experience as it is intimately perceived and lived, individuals cannot be reduced to *homunculi*, identified and described as models and statistics, as data and objective facts. The nature of literature itself is ambivalent, metaphoric and metonymic. It is able to express solidity and fluidity as well as homogeneousness and plurality, the smoothness and even the 'acrid, rough and crunchy'[2] nature of our existences. We not only lack the words to say who we are and what we want, but we are also spoon-fed, gorged and saturated by words which are as empty and lifeless as they are glitteringly attractive and seductive – the ubiquitous words that are repeated by the sirens of celebrity, used for amazing, new hi-tech devices and the latest irresistible must-have products which allow us to take our place in society in the way we are expected to.

And so, 'if you wish to cooperate with your readers in their urge (conscious or not) to find the truth of their own way of being-in-the-world and learn about the alternatives which lie unexplored, overlooked, neglected or hidden',[3] it is essential that sociology and literature work together to increase our capacity to judge and reveal the authenticity which is obscured by the veils that surround us, and to provide the freedom to follow our needs.

I had been thinking of calling this new series of conversations *Sister Literature* (even if the title will be *In Praise of Literature* – all things considered, not so different from my original idea) in recognition of the considerations in your last book, whose aim is summarized above and at the heart of all your sociological work, which has always been nurtured by literature. It is also a title partly inspired by two books written by friends of mine who tried, in different ways, to demonstrate how literature is extraordinary in making sense of our existences and the events of our time that we experience together.[4]

Naturally, the idea of the original title is also partly due to my own inclination, since I graduated a long time ago with a thesis on *Oedipus* by Marcel Proust and I had wanted to go to Paris to study with Lacan. It took getting to know and love your work in the early 1990s for me to enhance my awareness and my view of society without losing sight of the individuals who form it.

I would like you therefore to pursue your enlightened sociological reflections primarily as a narrative author, of course, but also using psychoanalysis or other human sciences because the partitions which divide these disciplines are anything but impervious.

In your latest book, *What Use Is Sociology?*,[5] you take pains to underline from the first chapter the primary importance of using the right words to describe reality. For example, you note that, in your distinct way of looking at sociology as a conversation with human experience, the English language is an obstacle because it does not have two separate words to describe 'experience'. These do exist in German: *Erfahrung*, meaning objective aspects of experience, and *Erlebnis*, meaning subjective aspects of experience.

The task of a sociologist with the necessary imagination to fulfil it is to expand the reach of the *Erlebnisse* and bring people out of their shells ('like ships in their bowls / they're in their melody', to use Mario Luzi's words)[6] to realize that many of the experiences they live individually, as if they were unique, are actually generated socially and can be manipulated (replacing 'with the aim of' with 'because of'). The sociologist has to expand his/her scope by submitting the *Erfahrungen* to a similar assessment. These objective experiences are like the market which, as Coetzee clarifies, was not made by God or the Spirit of History but rather by us human beings and therefore it is possible to 'unmake and remake it in a more acceptable way'.[7] These experiences can themselves be changed by taking a more critical and active role. Sometimes everything can take a lead from an authentic understanding of the words we use to describe our life and the world which surrounds us.

I have the impression that words in our liquid-modern world are under increasing pressure. As you point out, not only is their number falling but the words are also being shortened and reduced to a series of consonants in electronic messages which are now the increasingly dominant vehicle of communication. But even the words which continue to be pronounced fully are tending to be merged into a smaller area and chosen for emotional-hedonistic reasons. Clicking through the channels aimed at young people on television, such as MTV, M20 and DJ Television, the most striking visual aspects are the images of half-naked bodies, male and female, scrupulously representing a variety of ethnic groups to ensure the fig leaf of political correctness is preserved. But the ear is struck by the incessant repetition of a few key words: party, dance, sex, drink, night, fun. Pop music has always revolved around descriptions of love, predominantly the unhappy kind, so that ordinary people can easily identify with the ordinary lyrics. Any aliens watching 'youth' TV today and observing the scenes would think earthlings do nothing other than dance, get drunk and have sex, mostly at night, in an unrestrained and flamboyant frenzy. Obviously, if you consider the precarious nature of, and dearth of opportunity in, the lives of our children, the evidence provided by television is worse than antiphrasis, it is completely misleading.

The vocabulary of youth has been impregnated with an equally dangerous disease: the relentless spread of phrases that are simplified to the bone, ready-made so that everyone can sing them or decipher them even when their knowledge of English is very modest. It would certainly be a positive development if all non-Anglophones were able to master the basic vocabulary of what has become the 'language of communication', but the terminology in the lyrics of these songs is more than just basic, it is so skimpy and shrivelled as to become a sort of zero-grade verbalization, which is as monotonous as it is compartmentalized with words designed to penetrate the mental fabric of the kids, to invade their imagination, colonize their tastes and preferences, and dictate the direction of their enjoyment. For some months now, whenever a new song is released – such as 'Roar' by Katy Perry or 'Bonfire Heart' by James Blunt – for several weeks the video shows only the words of the song instead of images. This is to ensure a karaoke-like experience to ensure everyone can learn them quickly and easily. Only once they have been learned can the cheerful verbal barrage of banality give way to the images, which contain varying degrees of salaciousness, comical adventurousness in Katy Perry's 'Roar', and star a well-meaning motorcyclist in 'Bonfire Heart'. Apart from the subdued and saccharine tone of the messages in these songs – or, as happens in other cases, the energetic and unrestrained erotic charge – what is most striking is the erosion, withdrawal and dilution of the language.

The oversimplification of language echoes the oversimplification of music, as Milan Kundera poetically complained in a book translated from Czech in 1978, *The Book of Laughter and Forgetting*.[8] The writer had been excited by the twelve-tone innovations of Schoenberg, who managed to rethink music in an audacious way, but it has been followed by a creative wasteland which, rather than being silent, pours out endlessly cheesy music everywhere:

Schoenberg died, Ellington died but the guitar is eternal. The stereotype harmony, the banal melody, the rhythm

---

which is as insisted as it is monotonous, this is all that is left of music in this eternity of sounds. Everyone can feel united by the simple combinations of notes because it is like they are together shouting jubilantly, 'I am here!'. There is no more fragrant and unanimous communion than simple, shared existence. In this world, the Arabs can dance with the Jews and the Czechs with the Russians, bodies move in time with the rhythm of the notes, inebriated with the awareness of existing. That is why no work by Beethoven has been lived with the same collective passion as the hits churned out on a guitar.[9]

It is the same with words; they have been reduced to a mass of throw-away slogans. The progressive decline of the most important medium for articulating our vision of the world, without being hostage to received ideas, is truly frightening.

How can we free language from the grips of this spiral which is dragging it towards a deceitful and deadly Land of Toys?

Zygmunt Bauman   Be it Katy Perry or Marcel Proust and Lacan who would have something important to say about the unconscious premises of their consciousness – or you and I with all the rest of their readers or listeners – whatever we all and any of us see, think of seeing, or believe we are seeing, and whatever we do as a consequence, is woven in discourse.

'We live in discourse as fish live in water' – so suggests David Lodge in his latest novel[10] through the mouth of the hero, Desmond Bates – a man of many weaknesses, but a linguist of rather impeccable knowledge and feel of both *langue* and *parole* (two concepts coined by

Ferdinand de Saussure, and elaborated by Claude Lévi-Strauss, to denote, respectively, the system of language and its uses):

> Systems of law consist of discourse. Diplomacy consists of discourse. The beliefs of the great world religions consist of discourse. And in a world of increasing literacy and multiplying media of verbal communication – radio, television, the Internet, advertising, packaging, as well as books, magazines and newspapers – discourse has come more and more to dominate even the non-verbal aspects of our lives.

Indeed, we eat discourse, we drink discourse, we look at discourse, 'we even have sex by enacting the discourses of erotic fiction and sex manuals', Bates concludes; and – by the way – Lodge confirms, Riccardo, your observation that 'pop music has always revolved around descriptions of love [. . .] so that ordinary people can easily identify with the ordinary lyrics', when he adds that Professor Bates threw a reference to sex into his above-quoted welcoming speech to his first-year students in order 'to capture the attention of even the most bored and sceptical student'.

Lodge/Bates was right in this – as he was in all other parts of his laudation of linguistics. We are indeed made by discourse and live by it. It is discourse that sets us free; and it is discourse that sets the limits to our freedom and spurs us to transgress and transcend limits – already set, or yet to be set in the future. Discourse is that by which we are made while making it. And it is due to discourse, and its endemic urge to peep beyond the boundaries it draws to its freedom, that our being-in-the-world is a process of a perpetual – unending and infinite – becoming: our becoming, and our *Lebenswelt*'s becoming – becoming together, mixing though not gelling, tightly and inseparably plaited and braided and sharing our respective successes and misfortunes, tied to each other for better or worse – since the moment of our simultaneous conception and until death do us part.

What we call 'reality' when falling into a philosophical mood, or 'the facts of the matter' when we obediently follow the prompts of the *doxa*, is woven of words. No other reality is accessible to us: not the past 'wie es ist eigentlich gewesen' ('as it really happened'), which Leopold von Ranke famously called/ instructed his fellow nineteenth-century historians to recover. Commenting in his *Une rencontre*[11] on Juan Goytisolo's story of an old man, Milan Kundera points out that biography – any biography attempting to be what its name suggests it should – is, and cannot but be, an artificial, contrived logic imposed retrospectively on an incoherent succession of images, hoarded in memory in bits and pieces; and he concludes that, in a stark opposition to common-sense presumptions, the past shares with the future the incurable bane of unreality – stubbornly dodging/eluding, as they both do, the logic-driven nets woven of words. And yet this unreality is the only reality to be caught and had by us, 'living in discourse as fish in water'.

That unreal, all too unreal reality, we call 'experience'. We try hard, though with but mixed success, to glide over the suspicion of a falsehood lying-in-wait in the discourse of *Erfahrung* (of what happened to us); we cannot but admit that suspicion and worry about it when it comes to reporting an *Erlebnis* (how we lived through that happening). In both cases, we strive to pierce through the wall made of words and to the staunchly inaccessible land of 'wie es ist eigentlich gewesen'. Paradoxically though, that wall is interpretation: product of a processing meant to make sense of *Erfahrungen* and *Erlebnisse*, rendering them thereby fit for storage in memory and for reporting on demand, while preventing us from acting on our suspicions regarding their worthiness. The wall is built of words, but so is the sole battering ram available for its shattering. To deploy Kundera's metaphor, we may say that piercing through the currently torn-up curtain reveals another curtain, still whole, thickset and seamlessly compact. Interpretation is always an act of reinterpretation; reinterpretation is always a bridgehead to another reinterpretation. What we call a-priori as well as a-posteriori 'reality' can only reach us in the wrapping of pre-interpretations. A 'raw', 'pristine', 'pure' and 'unalloyed' – indeed un-deformed, 'wie es ist eigentlich gewesen' – reality is a phantom, though a useful one, insofar as it also plays the role of a sort of a Bethlehem star showing us, routinely irritated by the glaring imperfection of language, the road to linguistic perfection and so, hopefully, to truth. The chosen destination may not be attainable, but its vision prods us to move and to keep moving.

Human experience arrives at the workbenches of writers and sociologists alike in an already pre-interpreted form. Both literature and sociology are exercises in the 'secondary hermeneutic' – reinterpretation of the already interpreted. Both therefore need to engage in tracing the hidden seams along which the curtains of interpretation can be torn, and none can avoid revealing more curtains hidden behind those that they currently take apart. We are indeed, as you suggest, 'two sisters'.

I would take one more step and suggest that literature and sociology are not just ordinary sisters, but Siamese twins – and such Siamese twins as are, due to sharing their nourishing and digesting organs, surgically inseparable. As *sisters*, we are prone to engage in sibling rivalries; as *Siamese twin* sisters, however, we are bound to stop well short of parting our ways and are doomed to share in the same undertakings and to coordinate our moves.

Sharing our tasks, we cannot but share also our concerns; nor can we avoid being forced to face up to the same problems. As to the problems we share: due to the principal non-finality of all and any interpretation, and the seemingly incurable friability of the foundations on which they rest, they tend to be as confusing and baffling as they are grave, and utterly unlikely to allow for uncontentious resolutions. Interpretations of human experience are seldom innocuous: neutral to human interests and free from effects on human conduct. They are seldom if ever reliably insured against having unwelcome side effects and perpetrating collateral damages. For that reason, they may be – and, indeed, all too often are – resented – explicitly rejected or desisted – however strong their credentials might be on the ground of empirical evidence – whether by 'lay', that is commonsensical, wisdom, or by knowledge claiming to be superior because of its pretence to suprapersonality, scientific valour, value-free authority. The proposed resolutions to the shared problems are almost certainly bound to stay in what Alfred North Whitehead dubbed an 'essentially contested' condition. An unquestionable, universally recognized authority is in principle unattainable for either literature or sociology: another aspect of the 'elective kinship', or affinity, between the two approaches to the exploration of the human, all too human, mode of being-in-the-world.

Indeed, disinterestedness and value-neutrality, a status of independence from human, all too human, conflicts and antagonisms of interests and cognitive perspectives, are decidedly beyond the reach of either literature or sociology. The stratagems most commonly deployed to bypass this inconvenient truth (the insistence that aesthetic quality is the sole value by which art products need to be judged whatever their social, political or any other human consequences, by design or by default, could be – in the case of literature; or the insistence that the sole criterion by which the presentation of social realities could be evaluated is just how strictly their authors followed the established, professionally approved, methods of investigation – in the case of sociology) may placate some guilty consciences and/or help the culprits to wash their hands of their responsibility for the outcomes of their deeds – and yet, instead of insuring the two endeavours against a real (all too real) threat of perhaps unanticipated, yet all the same deeply harmful and morbid, consequences in their products, they only sweep the problem under the carpet, rendering its resolution yet more difficult – indeed unattainable. The two attempts to design and promote a public policy that, once accepted and systematically applied, would definitely remove the problem from the public agenda (proclaiming the free expression and promotion of views and opinions an inalienable part of universal human rights, and its opposite: denial of tolerance to the enemies of tolerance) involve their authors and followers in an endless chain of contradictions; they open

Pandora's boxes – each having one of its own – of again essentially contested, and in fact irresolvable, issues, whenever their practical application is attempted.

'In April 2009, PEN Slovakia, an organization which campaigns on behalf of the persecuted writers and in favour of free expression, issued a statement condemning the publication in a Slovakian journal of a poem by Radovan Karadžić', as Heather McRobie informs in her book *Literary Freedom*, published by Zero Books.[12] McRobie points out that both policies, however contradictory with each other, have their valid justifications and so need to be deployed simultaneously:

> If we conceptualize of the writer–society relationship as a symbiotic one, the flipside to the necessity of 'protecting the writer from society' (that is, protecting the writer from both censorship and the kind of self-censorship outlined by Orwell) would be 'protecting society from the writer', in instances where a writer's work could cause tangible damage to disadvantaged groups – namely, through literary hate speech.

Radovan Karadžić stands accused of incitement to racial hatred and, more generally, 'predominance of imagery relating to militarized and ritualized violence, purity, cleansing and ethnic superiority' – which provides grounds for classifying his poetry as a case of 'hate speech'. But, in his case, the 'hate speech' is associated with hateful and gory deeds: a documentary directed by Paul Pawlikowski (*Serbian Epics*, 1992) shows Karadžić on the top of a hill reciting his poetry while firing down on to Sarajevo. Can you apply both policies to such a case? Or should we admit their irreconcilability and decide which of the two ought to be given priority

when in conflict? McRobie plays down the magnitude
of the dilemma by suggesting that only 'hate speech',
an explicit 'incitement to racial hatred . . . or genocide',
provides a legitimate case for suspending the policy of
a universal right to expression, and qualifies that case
yet more by making its legitimacy (and illegitimacy)
'context-bound': 'The idea of context allows us to
modify our definition of hate speech, meaning that even
if we support censoring ultranationalist or Fascistic
art, we do not need to censor it in all contexts.' Where
ought the line to be drawn, though? And who is entitled
to draw it? And who has the reason and will to grant
him that right, and why, or to deny the right of line-
drawing? Indeed, Pandora's box is all but bottomless.

As, for instance, Katharine Gelber, a professor of
Public Policy at the University of Queensland, observes
in her article 'We Should Not Take Freedom For
Granted':

> At a very general level, Australians will say that they
> believe that free speech is important, and that they believe
> that we have it. Yet when you scratch the surface, the con-
> sensus fractures, and fractures relatively easily. People are
> willing to trample on free speech rights where it matters –
> at the coalface of political and community disputes. There
> are numerous examples of this.[13]

And let me note that, as a matter of fact, 'hate speech'
is a relatively rare and marginal incident among the
reasons for the right-to-speech violation. Much more
common and potentially no less harmful to human
freedom – even if obliquely rather than explicitly –
are SLAPP suits ('Strategic Lawsuits Against Public
Participation'): 'when corporations direct civil lawsuits

for defamation, negligence or nuisance against individuals and groups campaigning against their activities'. Those corporations 'are well resourced and have time at their disposal. They tend to make initially very large claims for damages, sometimes in millions of dollars . . . These suits are designed not to win damages from individuals and groups who typically do not have money, but to stop the campaigners' speech.'[14]

Which brings me, as I see it, to the crucial issue crying to be paid particularly acute attention when it comes to 'protecting society from the writer'. That issue is not so much the case of person/time-bound instances of conflict between public good and individual freedom, however spectacularly dramatized by the media and however privileged is the access granted them to the limelight of the public scene and so to public attention – as the subterranean, surreptitious, all too often toned-down and camouflaged, slow and gradual, and apparently innocuous and unnoticeable to many (as well as played down by many more still) erosion of public morale by ideas potentially devastating to social cohesion, mutual tolerance and solidarity, civilized cohabitation and mutual acceptance of different modes of being human. And let me declare right away that an effective protection of society against such ills becomes ever more a pipe dream – given the facile, uncontrolled access to the public arena offered by the Internet and universally accessible informatics technology, combined with impunity-guaranteed anonymity for its users. Suggestions that such policies can be devised and made effective are relics of the era of gatekeepers guarding the few available entries to the public sphere – though grow ever more hallucinatory as the public debate, increasingly conducted electronically, becomes a free-for-all, catch-as-you-catch-can zone. Rendering access to public-opinion-making largely independent from the selective policies of the big press, radio and TV corporations might be an enormous step forward in the fight for unconstrained freedom of expression (protecting writers from society), but it makes the protection of society from 'hate speech', its spread and normalization, its public acceptance and its gruesome, all too often macabre, effects an ever more doomed undertaking.

On 8 February 1975, Susan Sontag published in the *New York Review of Books* an article that deserves to be read again and again, as all the phenomena against which Sontag warned remain today as – if not yet more – salient, vigorous and topical as they presented themselves forty years ago to its author.[15] The immediate reason for writing the article was the sudden, in many ways baffling, rehabilitation of Leni Riefenstahl, an enthusiastic Nazi collaborator, and a close personal friend and admirer, as well as a pampered ward, of Hitler and Goebbels – and her restoration to the grace, admiration and favour of the American – and not only American – intellectual salons. Sontag reminds her forgetful readers that, far from being a naïve and innocent artist accidentally strayed into a wrong kind of company (victim of a misadventure akin to that which prompted Lenin to describe G. B. Shaw, a playwright whom he admired, as a decent man who strayed among the Fabians, whose politics he hated), Riefenstahl was in fact an incipient Nazi well *avant la lettre*; Siegfried Kracauer correctly described her film production preceding the Nazi ascent to power as 'an anthology of proto-Nazi sentiments'. Let me add that Sontag could include among the reasons to be wary the synchronic rehabilitation of Martin Heidegger or Carl Schmitt – and indeed of Friedrich Nietzsche; to the thoughts and deeds of all three of them, Kracauer's formula fits as flawlessly as it did to the oeuvre of Riefenstahl. Of the grim and daunting causes of the mysterious resurrection of the latter, Sontag opines: 'Riefenstahl's films are still effective because, among other reasons, their longings are still felt, because their content is a romantic ideal to which many continue to be attached':

> it is generally thought that National Socialism stands only for brutishness and terror. But this is not true. National Socialism – or, more broadly, Fascism – also stands for an ideal, and one that is also persistent today, under other banners: the ideal of life as art, the cult of beauty, the fetishism of courage, the dissolution of alienation in ecstatic feeling of community.

One of the 'larger themes of Nazi Ideology', which resonated harmoniously with the spirit and ambiance of Riefenstahl's creations (and, let me add, also with the increasingly popular mindset, abetted and beefed up by the media and the consumerist markets of our times) was 'the contrast between the clean and the impure, the incorruptible and the defiled, the physical and the mental, the joyful and the critical'. Herself, Riefenstahl announced in her interview for *Cahiers du Cinéma*: 'I am fascinated by what is beautiful, strong, healthy, what is living. I seek harmony.' Aren't we – and don't we – all?

I feel, however, that something of supreme importance was missing from the list of values and cults combining in the 'anthology of proto-Nazi sentiments':

the myth of the miraculously ennobling, refreshing, regenerating powers of violence, combat and war. While it is true that Nazism did not stand only for brutishness and terror, there is little doubt that the acquittal and unleashing of brutal terror was one of the main attractions – and probably the principal one – that drew the humiliated and browbeaten, dispossessed, disabled and vengeful masses to its ranks.

Our twin/Siamese sisters have, it seems, a horrendously awesome task on their hands. All too often we console ourselves that the currently prevailing symbolic violence, however immoral and cruel, is still a welcome advance on that which dominated the last century. Some psychologists add to that consolation assurances that exposure to images of violence unloads (and in a relatively innocuous form), rather than beefing up, the aggressive impulses that for one reason or another accumulate over time, threatening a carnal and much more gory explosion – and provides the occasion to collectively release the supplies of unspent aggression (as in, for instance, the recent World Cup matches, those festive carnivals of 'us or them' gladiatorial combats that seem to follow the ancient-Roman 'panem et circenses' recipe for keeping the drained-of-steam plebeians meek and obeisant on their weekdays). I joined the uncounted millions watching with bated breath the spectacles of unashamed physical violence – pushing and pulling, tripping each other up – all followed invariably by comedies of shrewdly pretended innocence and displays of outrage at false accusations. I joined people entertained with a long series of knock-outs, the joys of knocking out and the humiliation of the knocked-out; and I found the messages flowing from millions of TV screens around the world somewhat at odds with such assurances. The most obvious of the messages, likely to settle firmly in the dungeons of the unconscious as well as to find its way into the toolbox of the art-of-life practitioners, was something like 'Everything goes if only you manage to emerge scot-free and avoid any penalty.' A powerful and insidious lesson indeed – though not the one that education-for-life is called upon to convey and deliver. We must do something to prevent the world which we daily shape and are shaped by from being made to the measure of the life-strategies that lesson suggests.

Splitting of the known part of the globe into 'us' vs 'them' is at least as old as the human species, though I believe that it is much older than that. But who is 'us' and who 'them' has, as a rule, a much shorter pedigree, being a product of the time-bound cultural recycling of the durable stuff of nature. The particular recycled product that found its latest, 2014 application in the purpose-built Brazilian stadiums was conceived, as I already explained elsewhere, in 1555 in Augsburg, with the idea of putting an end to the seemingly endless, while increasingly gory, massacres of religious wars; born in Münster and Osnabrück in 1648, having been baptized on that occasion as 'cuius regio, eius religio'; confirmed 200 years later, in the year that went down in history as that of the 'Spring of Nations', under a name slightly altered through squeezing 'natio' into the place vacated by 'religio'. It was offered a planet-wide realm by Woodrow Wilson, presiding over the Versailles Peace Conference convened during the interval in the thirty-year-long planet-wide massacre of nations. Almost 100 years later it was replayed in front of the planet-wide

TV network as a piece of planet-wide entertainment. Is that how the four-centuries-long story of that particular cultural recycling of the 'us' vs 'them' scission, that tale full of sound and fury, is about to end? Not with a bang but with a whimper? Or perhaps, with its evil-doing powers as yet not quite exhausted, that particular cultural product won't stop at its to-date achievement, measured by hundreds of millions of dead soldiers and as many widows and orphans, nor settle for breaking the legs or ribs of 'enemy' footballers? Perhaps what we see is but an exercise in keeping the powder of emotions dry – a training for big matches played on world-wide battlefields instead of the world's stadiums?

2

Salvation through Literature

Riccardo Mazzeo Yesterday morning I went to meet an author, Eraldo Affinati, whose latest book *Elogio del ripetente*[1] ('In Praise of the Repeating Student') made me think of you and something you wrote in the preface to your book *Collateral Damage*.[2] The underlying theme was almost disarming, in its obvious transparency. You have observed several times how things right in front of us can often remain unperceived. You wrote:

> The moment an electrical power circuit becomes over-loaded, the first part to go bust is the fuse [. . .] the *least resistant* part [. . .] A bridge does not break down and collapse once the load it carries transcends the average strength of its spans: it collapses much earlier, the moment the weight of the load goes over the carrying capacity of *one* of its spans – its *weakest*.[3]

You explain why engineers and maintenance operators have to be attentive and accurate in the design and testing stage because carelessness is only seen '*after* the disaster has struck: when it comes to counting the human victims of neglect and the exorbitant financial costs of restoration. One structure, however, stands out . . . *society*'.[4]

A society which measures itself by the average incomes within it and variables based only on consumption reduces the disqualified underclass to a life as bystanders: they become a sort of 'alien body [. . .]. Something not unlike a cancerous growth, whose most sensible treatment is excision, and short of that an enforced, induced and contrived confinement and/or remission.'[5]

As Richard Sennett wrote in his book *Together*,[6] most of this 'collateral damage' – these poor people – are already deeply aware of being just cannon fodder at school, so much so that they prefer gang affiliation to success at school or in the social environment. These unfortunates feature as the main characters in the book by Affinati. He is well known in Italy and has been translated into other languages (although not into English).

He chose to be transferred from the 'normal' secondary school where he taught to an extremely difficult environment at a vocational school where pupils were just one step away from exclusion from the academic system. It is as if he took to heart your teaching, according to which 'the explosive compound of growing social inequality and the rising volume of human suffering relegated to the status of "collaterality" (marginality, externality, disposability, not a legitimate part of the political agenda) has all the markings of being potentially the most disastrous among the many problems humanity may be forced to confront, deal with and resolve in the current century'.[7]

Affinati feels strongly the injustice of inequality. He

is profoundly aware that schools have been bureaucratized in that pass marks are set by equally applied criteria. This is supremely unfair: a pass mark for a student from a good family where fairy tales are read and children grow up amidst books, love and attention is much less of an achievement than it is for a child who had to fight tooth and nail for everything, whose parents are separated, pay little attention to their offspring, speak in dialect and set a bad example in their cultural void. That is why Affinati, along with other good teachers, chose to work with the weakest, the most defenceless and the most deprived. Often all that a student who has to repeat a year needs, to avoid his destiny of certain failure, is a simple change, a step, an idea that an alternative does exist: 'Anyone starting from the bottom only needs a little help to start moving up. They often refuse to budge even an inch but that is precisely why we need to recognize even the tiniest improvement. Certainly in his story the repeating student is not satisfied [. . .]. You need to reward the movement even before you see the results.'[8]

Affinati is the son of two illiterate orphans (his mother miraculously survived a concentration camp and his father was a street hawker) so he discovered the pleasure of literature by himself, buying cheap books from market stalls. He started by reading Hemingway, who provided him with the thrill of adventure, then he was charmed by Tolstoy and Dostoyevsky. He considers himself to have been lucky, but cannot help thinking about the girls and boys who are destined to a life without thinking (and consequently without the freedom to judge) and he realizes how important somebody acting on their behalf could be.

The teacher is a specialist of the inner adventure, the artisan of time, youth's card dealer. When teaching is well done, the students stay inside him and he always remembers them all, like little drummers who kept the beat on the bass drum of his existence. And the students never forget the teacher. They hold a memory as if he were a stand-in for their father: a stuntman who does the risky action scenes in the place of the main character. Saying 'no' does not necessarily meet with approval, but it is sometimes more important than continuing to say 'yes'. Nowadays children are left in an empty dialectic, one without obstacles to overcome. Their teachers are the only ones able to remind them of the value of being serious, austere and concentrated in a society which privileges beauty, health and wealth.[9]

Inspiring a love in one's students for books in their environment seems to be an anachronistic and irreconcilable stubbornness, almost something to be ashamed of for whoever strives for it. It is extremely arduous and has to be done in uncomfortable, almost painful conditions, as it was for Lorenzino, a deprived pupil:

> His first readings are like fires lit in the Antarctic, they do not warm nor create affinities, they are extinguished straightaway leaving him alone. He takes on novels as if he was the first man on the planet to do so, with no one to share them with. They seem like uncut diamonds which the repeating student keeps in a pocket touching them every so often for reassurance they are still there. He avoids talking about them to friends.[10]

Enlightenment can happen after being able to identify with a person or an experience, as happened with little Sonia, a Polish girl, whose smile was as big as her aversion to reading. After listening to her teacher read one of the *Kolyma Tales*, 'The Carpenters', by the great Russian writer Varlam Shalamov, and hearing the experiences of the prisoners in a Gulag camp who tried to calculate exactly how cold it was, she was reminded of her grandfather whose legs were always freezing during the war.

The go-between has to be ready to treat the pupils as subjects and not as objects so they work together, all get their hands dirty and accept the risk that disputes may even become physical. Just like Affinati, who, when faced with a jeering class that was in complete turmoil, went immediately to confront the ringleader, or like Pope Francis who, when he was archbishop in Buenos Aires, often went to the shantytowns, known as *villas miserias*, alone, unannounced and on foot, to chat with his people.

> Ramon Antonio Garcia is one of the many invisibles in Buenos Aires. He survives driving a *remis*, a shabby car that becomes a taxi when required. He provides a service to those few adventurers who want to take a trip through the shantytowns that surround the city [. . .]. They are usually journalists or tourists hoping to look around the hardest and most obscure parts of Baires. They call Garcia because it is too risky to enter a *villa* alone. 'Because down here', he says, 'life has little value and there is always someone ready to kill for a handful of pesos'. That is why Garcia was left speechless when he saw Bergoglio. He had been unaware that the cardinal archbishop of Buenos Aires behaved like that.[11]

Pope Francis was a teacher too. In the 1970s, he worked in a college and was behind the formation of a band

which played Beatles songs and gave women the opportunity of taking part in theatre events organized there;
he also started a creative-writing course together with
Jorge Luis Borges. It shows how literature can really be
a path to salvation.

Zygmunt Bauman 'The teacher is a specialist of the
inner adventure, the artisan of time, youth's card dealer'
. . . How beautifully you've put it, how vividly and how
accurately. Hitting the bull's eye, indeed.

But what are the cards s/he, the teacher, deals? These
cards are, as Amartya Sen and Martha Nussbaum
would say, 'capabilities':[12] skills and inclinations that
constitute the necessary, perhaps also the sufficient,
conditions of a decent and dignified, productive and
gratifying life – such as, among others, sensibility (eyes
and ears wide open to the world's sights and sounds, to
what it can offer, to others who inhabit it, to what they
might offer, and to what they need in order to be able
to deliver on their promise); imagination and thought
(above all, the ability to deploy both, to discern between
options and choose between them, as well as muster
enough determination to hold to such choices, and act
on them and see them through); emotions (ability to
love, to care for others, while resenting and fighting
back the evils of indifference, denigration, wrongdoing,
downgrading, denial of dignity and humiliation); practical reason (the ability to visualize a model of good
life, as well as to gather resolve to dedicate one's life
to its pursuit); sociability and the skills and the will of
association (the know-how needed to share life with
others and to live one's own life with the well-being of
others in mind – the desire and will to comprehend each

other's needs, values and attitudes, and readiness to negotiate a mutually satisfactory *modus vivendi* as well as to accept the self-limitations and self-sacrifices which such a *modus* may call for).

Society's 'weakest links', whom the hugely popular TV quiz series under the same title recommended the millions of its addicted watchers should disqualify, eliminate and exclude from the game, but whom Affinati chose to teach, suffer shortage of such capabilities and the absence of opportunity for their appropriation. They miss therefore what can be called the 'meta-capability': the capability of accessing the others and the very desire for such access. In most cases, those 'weakest links' are not aware of their loss, having no opportunity to appreciate the value of experience they've missed. What they hear from the public address systems of our thick-skinned and heartless consumerist society, and from other residents of 'mean districts' (spaces they have been cast in and the only ones they are allowed to inhabit) – from people already seduced by the siren songs they broadcast – is but the want-want-want, buy-buy-buy, dump-dump-dump message: call, allurement, guile and command rolled into one. As I noted three years ago, in the aftermath of the memorable London riots of the disqualified, frustrated and aggrieved 'flawed consumers' in the poor and run-down district of Lewisham:[13]

> From cradle to coffin we are all trained and drilled to treat shops as pharmacies filled with drugs to cure or at least mitigate all illnesses and afflictions of our lives and lives in common. Shops and shopping acquire thereby a fully and truly eschatological dimension. Supermarkets, as George

Ritzer famously put it, are our temples [. . .] I shop, therefore I am. To shop or not to shop, this is the question. [. . .]
For the anathematized, found wanting and banished by the
Church of Consumers, they are the outposts of the enemy
erected on the land of their exile. Those heavily guarded
ramparts bar access to the goods which protect others
from a similar fate [. . .] Steel gratings and blinds, CCTV
cameras, security guards at the entry and hidden inside
only add to the atmosphere of a battlefield and on-going
hostilities.

The bells sounding, day in, day out, from the bel-
fries of consumerist temples are loud, sonorous and
resonant. Plugging ears won't help; there is no hiding
from the deafening racket. The bell-ringers are not particularly choosy – bells are meant and hoped to draw
pilgrims from all walks of life (probably the sole equal-
ity granted, indiscriminately and wholeheartedly, to the
condition of all denizens of our society of consumers).
But inside the temple there is no altar or even a modest
chaplet dedicated to the glory of the Sen/Nussbaum
capabilities. Seekers of missing capabilities *lasciate ogni
speranza, voi ch'entrate* ('abandon all hope, you who
enter') – but on no account desist from visiting or strug-
gling hard to earn permission to enter. Visiting the
temple is a duty, not a right which one is free to pick
up or allow to lie idle. You might be refused entry by
the hosts and the guards they hire, if you fail the test,
falling short of acquitting yourself of the consumer's
duty, but no one has the right to opt out from attending
the services of their own will, or at least from earnestly
trying to attend. Those whom Affinati chose to teach
were the heretics of the Church of Consumers – though

not by their own choice, but by the verdict of the Holy Inquisition supervising the integrity of the Church.

In Vittorio de Sica's 1951 masterly film *Miracolo a Milano*, an old, wise and good-hearted woman, Lolotta, finds little Toto on a cabbage patch and places him in an orphanage. On his eighteenth birthday, Toto is let out from the orphanage and joins the homeless, poverty-stricken squatters marooned on a run-down, ramshackle and desolate plot near Milan. Lolotta offers him a wondrous gift: a magic dove able to fulfil whatever wishes anyone asks it to fulfil. Toto – a kindhearted and compassionate creature – invites his companions-in-misery to come forward with their wishes. What follows, however, is an unprepossessing spectacle of a fierce and unrelenting competition in 'one-upmanship' (scoring a point over and above the score obtained by another person); each pauper asks for one or two more fur coats than the preceding one had a moment ago been allotted, or twice as much money: whatever you got, I want to get more. When a huge deposit of oil is accidentally discovered on the plot, the squatters are rounded up, arrested and imprisoned to make room for an oil well. Then a real – and last – miracle in the story, the most miraculous of them all, occurs: to avoid incarceration and simultaneously escape their own greed, which – frustratingly – failed to make them happier, the squatters straddle broomsticks lent to them by the city-square sweepers, and fly away. Where to? Well, finding a destination, and the means of reaching it, must have been the most knotty part of the miracle.

What all that amounts to is that the odds in the currently prevailing kind of society are set against the acquisition, mastery and deployment of the capabilities whose possession, coupled with the capacity to use them, are, as Sen and Nussbaum convincingly argue, indispensable for a dignifying and gratifying human life. The odds are also against an equitable distribution of those capabilities. I would suggest that the stark inequality in the distribution of these particular goods currently lies at the foundation of social inequality in all its other dimensions. The cards which your ideal teacher ought to deal, or is bound to regardless, are in notoriously short supply. But goods like capabilities should've been, by their very nature, exempted from the game of supply and demand: after all, they tend to expand with consumption, instead of shrinking. As an old, albeit now all-but-forgotten American saying goes: if I give you a dollar and you give me a dollar we have one dollar each; if I give you a thought and you give me a thought each of us has two thoughts. The currently hegemonic consumerist syndrome, aided and abetted by the competitive markets in its job of entrenching the one-upmanship life strategy, has managed nevertheless to transform their acquisition and mastery into a zero-sum game.

I agree that an ideal teacher is able (and likely to try hard) to promote the human, all-too-human, capabilities under most unpromising, downright hostile circumstances. He may even succeed in some cases. Many Lorenzinos wait to be found in all sorts of 'mean districts', urban ghettoes, '*quartiers*' and '*favelas*', even if it never occurred to them to dream of being found by the likes of Affinati. But how many? And why, invariably, so few and far between? The place assigned to Lorenzinos of this world, in societies afflicted by extensive and multidimensional inequality, does not determine their fate; but it does manipulate the statistical probability of their choices and chances of success. The more Affinatis are around us, the more Lorenzinos are likely to be found and be encouraged and helped to lift themselves from their cruel fate. But there are limits to what Affinatis can do, if they confine themselves and their wards to the search for individual solutions to socially produced and endlessly reproduced problems. To exceed those limits, Affinati would need Toto's magic dove.

Yes, we may individually seek and individually find salvation in literature, or a film, a song, a painting – all those creations we embrace under the name of 'arts', meaning the works of imagination, able in its flight – just like Toto's impoverished and indolent squatters – to leave behind the harsh realities of its homeless home – that desolate waste requisitioned for an oil well. But to what practical effect?

3
The Pendulum and Calvino's Empty Centre

Riccardo Mazzeo In *What Use Is Sociology?*, you explain that the phases of pre-modernity (or the *ancien régime*), modernity and present-day liquid modernity are not, in actual fact, self-contained elements, since the incessant surfacing of one or another of these trends bears witness to their coexistence.

Working in education, one observation that came to mind about Jean Piaget's immense theory was the clean-cut *passing* of each stage in a child's development process. In Bruner, similar advances and shifts from the learning axis are defined – however, the change in the new phase is not so radical as to *wipe out* all previous ways of learning. In Freud too, moreover, although it is true that the oral stage is followed by the anal stage and then by the genital stage – which is the most mature – oral and anal impulses continue to *coexist* during the entire lifetime of a human being. Yet now you make me think that what happens at a psychological level also happens from a sociological perspective, and if I hadn't read you the thought would never have crossed my mind. In *What Use Is Sociology?*, when Keith Tester and Michael Hviid Jacobsen[1] ask you how relevant nostalgia is for you, you say that the progress of things in the world is not linear but moves like a pendulum, since something which existed before is necessarily missing from every new state of affairs, and one notices it is missing only *à fait accompli*, once the change has occurred. We are not therefore dealing with a feeling of nostalgia for what no longer exists and that we lament, but for the fact that on the one hand we notice it exclusively *ex post*, and on the other because it is a perfect, definitive construction condemned to remain forever illusory and in a state of becoming, with inescapable hybridity and melding. And it is for this reason, as you wrote in your conversations with Keith Tester from thirteen years ago, that you really liked 'Lyotard's wisecrack: you cannot be truly modern without first being postmodern'.[2]

Raymond Aron's daughter, the sociologist (and political scientist) Dominique Schnapper, raised in her latest book[3] the risks *Homo democraticus* runs in his current fundamentalist version of 'extreme democracy', which aspires to unlimited well-being even to the point of wanting to choose the rules one is to be subjugated to, even in institutional spheres like schools and justice. I am not talking about the (awful) *ad personam* laws that Berlusconi tailored for himself, but about unrestrained and excessive radical criticism, like that of the Five Star Movement, which has gone viral on the web. We are dealing with a generalized hysteria, which, with the passing of any kind of *Gemeinschaft*, capable of establishing individual freedom in relation to that of other members of the community – and with the passing of *Gesellschaft* too, due to the fortuitous metaphor of a society *imagined* in terms of a community but experienced as irrespective of a real and true community of individuals – leaves people powerless and at the same time, in contrived contrast, aloof.

Schnapper's book seems to be echoed by Moisés Naím's *The End of Power*.[4] It talks of micro-powers which are ever more capable of countering larger powers, especially thanks to the web. Marco Belpoliti talks about 'rebels, political fringe parties, innovative start ups, hackers, youths lacking popular leaders, new media and charismatic figures who seem to have popped up out of nowhere shaking down the old order'. And then there are Grillo, Casaleggio and their Five Stars, and Assange's Wikileaks. It reminds me of an article by Italo Calvino published in *Corriere della Sera* forty years ago, which ended with the words: 'Modern society tends towards an extremely complicated set-up, which gravitates towards an empty centre, and it is in this empty centre that all the powers and values gather.'[5]

I believe I hear an echo in these words of your description of the local stopovers which global powers need in order to refuel, and of the whirlwind of influences that crisscross each other without us being able to establish in advance which small or large source will wield the most influence in the construction of new and ever more precarious balances.[6] And an 'empty centre' is likewise evoked in a passage from your conversations with Keith Tester:

> I believe that the danger we will have to face in the 21st century will not be totalitarian coercion – the obsession of what has just happened – but the collapse of 'totality', capable of guaranteeing the autonomy of human society

[. . .] With hindsight, we are now painfully aware of the dangers that 'totality' brings with it when it is unleashed and runs amok.[7]

Zygmunt Bauman All and any variety of development, or of becoming, is a tangle of continuity and discontinuity. Every snapshot of a developing/becoming entity is a palimpsest of many layers, very few of them – if any – effaced and extinguished completely; most are either fully overlaid and hidden under a next coat of paint, or still shine through from beneath another stroke of the paintbrush; some of them may be relocated and incorporated into a different composition, or stored in a sort of Freudian 'unconscious' – currently (implying: momentarily) invisible, yet in principle recoverable. That applies to both macro- and micro-phenomena. The tangle is so dense and tight, that spotting the caesura justifying the verdict of discontinuity is as a rule 'essentially contested'; its acceptance is in the last account a matter of convention, permanently open to questioning and revision.

I believe that abandoning the old assumption of the principal and unmitigated opposition between continuity and discontinuity was part and parcel of another watershed shift in the story of human perception of the world – one described by Ilya Prigogine in his epoch-making study/manifesto under a title that says it all: *The End of Certainty*.[8] 'Classical science emphasized order and stability; now, in contrast, we see fluctuation, instability, multiple choices, and limited predictability at all levels of observation.' In the classical view, 'laws of nature express certitudes. When appropriate initial conditions are given, we can predict with certainty the future, or "retrodict" the past. Once instability is included, this is no longer the case, and the meaning of the laws of nature changes radically, for they now express possibilities or probabilities'; 'science is no longer identified with certitude and probability with ignorance'.[9]

To put all that in a lay, commonsensical perspective, we may say that the palimpsest in question is a multi-layer imprint of not so much immutable laws in operation, but choices made between possibilities; if we are lucky to have many instances available to scrutiny, it can be read out as well as the evidence of a statistically expressible distribution of probabilities. There is always a snag, though. With this new awareness, 'the equivalence between the individual and statistical levels is indeed broken'; 'generalization of dynamics (of aggregates) [. . .] cannot be expressed in terms of (individual) trajectories'. Individual trajectories 'are the outcomes of stochastic, probabilistic processes'.[10]

The difficulty we encounter in trying to separate the elements of continuity and discontinuity in the seamless flow of time is further exacerbated by the difficulty of sundering the outcomes of probabilistic processes from those ascribable to processes of a deterministic character. In a rather impressionistic mode, I suggested[11] a two-factorial analysis of the individual life trajectory: fate (or what 'happens to us' without consulting our preferences), the factor responsible for setting the range of realistic options; and character (what is by design or default an object of our making), a factor responsible for selection among the options – admitting, however, the near impossibility of cleanly separating the two intimately intertwined and interacting factors.

Piaget developed his theory of developmental phases while still in the era of chasing 'natural laws manifesting certitude' – more to the point, an era of building 'ideal types' that could be represented as unambiguously uniform and universal: traits which could not be found in a similarly 'pure' form in the objects of the empirical world – only in their idealizations abstracted from their natural settings. Trying, for instance, to comprehend why powerful minds insisted for so many centuries on assuming physical time to be reversible, whereas, as we now know, it is the irreversible-time processes that prevail in the universe, Prigogine points out that the pendulum – that crowning example of the physicists' reversible time and a phenomenon on which the assumption of time's reversibility rested – is but an imagined entity having no referents in the 'real world': one that could be conjured up only in an imaginary world in which friction had been suspended or from which it was entirely eliminated. The 'real world' fate, however, the factor that sets the stage for the choosing/selecting activity of a character to produce a life trajectory as their combined effect, is also time-bound: the subject of 'irreversible-time' processes. Some possibilities become less 'realistic' and so less likely to be selected, and so it is reasonable to suppose that the distribution of probabilities will alter its shape; to suppose otherwise would be akin to prognosticating the endless persistence of the friction-free pendulum in monotonous repetition of the same sequence of moves. But were the children investigated by Piaget in the same state (i.e., cast in the same aggregate of circumstances) as are the cohorts of children arriving nowadays in schools to be educated? How have the 'frictions' diverting the movements of the pendulum from their idealized model changed since Piaget completed his research?

I wouldn't pretend to compose an exhaustive roll-call of alterations, so here you are – just a few of them, chosen at random, albeit with an eye on those that have probably made a lot of change in the dialectics of fate and character, as well as in the nature of each of its two factors.

To start with: as noted by Arlie Russell Hochschild,[12] an indefatigable researcher of continuous change in the conditions under which contemporary selves are formed, 'the percentage of babies born to single mothers reached (in the U.S.) 40 percent by 2011, and studies revealed that half of American children spent at least part of their lives in single-parent households'. Nothing else could be expected, considering that 'in 1900, about 10 percent of marriages ultimately ended in divorce, while today, for first marriages, chances stand as 40 to 50 percent', whereas second and third marriages are both yet more frequent and happen faster. Hence the framework shaped by fate – or in this case a time-bound stage of irreversible cultural process, in which the objects of Piaget's study 'developed psychologically' – has changed well-nigh beyond recognition. The so-called 'latchkey kids' in a family home usually emptied of adults (a constantly growing sector of American children) are prime candidates for developing what Hochschild dubs 'outsourced selves': the kind of patchwork selves composed – loosely – from the (mostly purchasable) services offered by expert counsellors specializing in virtually every aspect of life. From a tender age, children tend to acquire and expand their dependence on market instructions, hoping to find there the goods needed for life and the ready-made recipes for their use. Authority

---

of the advice/guidance available on the market tends to be measured by their current market price. 'The greatest innovation', Hochschild suggests, 'are those services that reach into the heart of our emotional lives, a realm previously more shielded from the market'. The market 'has made inroads into our very understanding of the self. In the marketization of personal life, acts that were once intuitive or ordinary – deciding whom to marry, choosing a name for your newborn, even figuring out what to want – now require the help of paid experts'; 'personal experience can become a thing we purchase – the "perfect" date, birthday, wedding – detached from our part in creating it'.[13] Self-confidence, personal autonomy, use of an unprecedentedly wide assortment of individual freedoms cannot but suffer in consequence.

Another territory of vast and speedy change: in the times of the Internet, world-wide web and 'social' websites, and with the members of the young generation spending, spiritually and/or bodily, a half – if not more – of their waking time in the company of screens instead of humans, most socializing activity tends to shift from the face-to-face and eye-to-eye category to the electronically mediated. That shift cannot but run parallel with the decay of socializing skills, indispensable in the specifically human, all-too-human, mode of being-in-the-world. Online networks differ from offline communities by the facility, as well as inconvenience-and-discomfort-free mode, of their operation; for the same reason, however, the electronically set and sustained inter-human bonds are notorious for their frailty, while the masters of composing tweets and exchanging messages are likely to be growingly inept in the – as difficult as it is imperative – art of dialogue.

4
The Father Problem

Riccardo Mazzeo How the figure of the father has changed in today's world has been explained with great persuasiveness by the psychoanalyst Massimo Recalcati who, taking inspiration from the teachings of Lacan, has described the 'evaporation of the father' in books like *Cosa resta del padre? La paternità nell'epoca ipermoderna* ('What Remains of the Father? Fatherhood in the Hypermodern Era'), *Il complesso di Telemaco* ('The Telemachus Complex') and *Patria senza padri* ('Fatherland Without Fathers'). I already mentioned this to you in *On Education* and I'm sure we'll pick up the discussion again later on, but here I would like to draw your attention to how little the old model of a father as an authoritative figure survives today, lurking, unnoticed, unaware, in fathers who are weak, infantilized or absent. Essentially, what is left of the fathers of long ago – cruel maybe, but present – in the faded misfits who have become today's fathers?

A great Italian Jungian analyst, Luigi Zoja, tried to explain this in, from my point of view, his most important book, *Il gesto di Ettore*[1] ('Hector's Gesture'), and he does it by building on the well-known humiliation Freud's father was subjected to when he couldn't pluck up the courage to face up to the adversary who had thrown his fur hat into the mud, and on the consequences this tale had for Sigmund. The father of psychoanalysis understood and forgave his father only when he read the *Aeneid* and understood Aeneas' reasons for putting the continuity of the family and of his people before the honour of defending himself in battle, and he was grateful to Virgil for the peace which this led to with his father, resulting in his book *The Interpretation of Dreams* starting with a verse from one of his father's works.

The problem is that whilst a mother who lets herself be humiliated will never be rejected by her child, if a father lets himself be insulted he may hear from his child that 'he is not behaving like a father', and that the child needs to feel 'his father is close to him not only with fairness and love but also with strength: because relationships in society are made up not only of love, nor only of justice, but of brute strength too':[2] 'Western tradition often prefers an unfair father who is a winner to the rest of the world to a fair father considered to be a loser: this paradox is well known to Shakespeare, who created in *King Lear* the prototype of a father who is rejected when he loses his strength and prestige.'[3]

We have seen that one of the consequences of the movement of 1968 was a weakening of fathers' aggressiveness: the model of the authoritative father was challenged by that generation, and consequently fathers felt they had to abandon this domineering aggressiveness with their children, opting for an approach as a gentle, understanding friend. But we have also seen how the children of weak fathers tend to look for 'strong' father figure substitutes amongst the bullies of their neighbourhood: 'A father's authority has become democratized and its strength has in many ways been dissolved; but our subconscious cannot eliminate in a few generations what has dominated it for millennia. Despite lacking in fathers, despite probably being in transition towards a new order, Western society, at least subconsciously, remains a patriarchal one.'[4]

In *A Natural History of Evil*,[5] you pointed out how individuals or populations struck by terrible catastrophes receive aid which is not, however, prone to last over time: if distressing conditions last too long, others pull away from the victims with a sort of annoyance which becomes less and less concealed, and, regarding the figure of the father, 'it is difficult to overcome the repulsion that losers stir up, especially when they have also lost their dignity'.[6]

But how was this paternal authority won, before we lost it? Zoja talks about the frenzy early humans displayed when facing animals, which got bigger and bigger, continuing their voyage of discovery until 'the psyche really expanded and imitated the nature it was superimposing itself on; then it chose self-containment, putting in place an internal balancing mechanism; then it assigned itself both the river and the river bank'.[7] Their sexual activity was excessive but, precisely because human young were the most defenceless, in order to protect them the monogamous family arose a long time ago.

[P]olygamists cancelled out each other's genetic characteristics in blood and even when they survived they risked being expelled from their communities for being too violent.

The others, however, were the future dominators of the universe, because they had been able to suppress immediate gratification of instincts – the aggressive instinct towards rivals, the sexual instinct towards females – in favour of a planned life: fuller but not immediate. This is a pedestal of paternal qualities.[8]

This ability to join moral forces – deferring enjoyment in favour of the sacrifice needed to build and consolidate the well-being of one's family and one's country – with material forces to be used against one's enemies reached its peak with the well-known 'puritan' praised by Max Weber, about whom you wrote memorable pages in *Legislators and Interpreters*.[9]

You dedicate a large portion of that book to your recognition of the Enlightenment, when intellectuals still held their roles as 'legislators' who dictated the agenda to 'enlightened despots' and had not yet been downsized into the role of 'interpreters' in a multi-focal environment where theories abounded – something still true today – and where none of them prevails enough to be considered 'the truth'. Today there are 'truths' which vie with each other, and Zoja notes how the crisis of authority started with the Enlightenment. It is a curious fact that both heralds of the French Revolution, Voltaire and Rousseau, had complicated relationships with their own fathers: the father of the first disowned him, and the father of the second wasn't capable of being a real father to his children: 'in the behaviour of a symbolic individual, a collective image is hidden. A father's gift has always been the public recognition of his child; the other possibility was disownment, again in the hands of the father. Voltaire looked for a real alternative: if recognition or disownment is a choice, it can come from the child too.'[10]

So, whilst in Paris in the eighteenth century the most progressive women emancipated themselves from the condition of being 'classic' mothers by leaving their children with wet nurses, and threw themselves into reading and salon conversations, 'Voltaire fought with the father he had on the outside and he tore him off; Rousseau with the one he had inside of him.'[11]

Since that moment, the crisis of the father has continued to worsen: with industrialization and the transition of the peasant father – who, despite being tyrannical, was well rooted in his role – into the factory-worker father – who, along with proximity, also loses his hold on his children, who in turn see him return home drunk in the evening, and watch him, spent, in front of a blaring TV – and finally into the father of today, whose authority is ever more eroded: 'Being richer in objects and poorer in psychology we do not understand that a mystery may make more sense and be more intense than its solution. Men have resigned as fathers by refusing the symbolic dimension.'[12] So, in the maternal world in which we live, where we look for salvation in gurus or in psychotherapists' offices, an open fissure or abyss remains in our children: 'We cannot exclude the fact that, just as [we] looked for dictatorship because [we] were hungry for a father figure, our search for a father includes a secret nostalgia for dictatorship. The insecurity which today brings us to seek out a father figure is nevertheless a psychic relative of that which brought us to tyrants.'[13]

In the end, the litmus test for Zoja's reflections is in the alleged autonomy of the 'direct democracy' of the Five Star Movement, from which the absolute dictator Beppe Grillo purges anyone who abstains from absolute obedience. What is your opinion on this?

Zygmunt Bauman I suppose that Lacan and Calvino (like Nietzsche half a century earlier, when announcing the death of God) were trying to penetrate the essence of the same process, only using different entries and reporting what they found in different idioms. That process means, to recall Calvino, being drawn by the centripetal force of the maelstrom of contemporaneity to a centre spattered by corpses of the many who aspired in the past to settle there – yet otherwise void. The corpse that caught Lacan's attention was the figurehead of the Father; for Nietzsche, it was the Father of all Fathers – God; for numerous others, the Fatherland.

God, Father, Fatherland are different names given to a totality greater than the sum of its (individual!) parts – Hobbes' Leviathan, Durkheim's society, Carl Schmitt's Sovereign. Schmitt showed himself to be the most perceptive and sober among them in titling his magnum opus *Political Theology*, and defining the figure of the 'Sovereign' not so much by his prerogative and capacity of law-making, but by the unaccountability for law-breaking that grounds both acts – making laws and breaking them – solely in his decision; in the last instance, the sovereign is he who owes the subjects of his rule neither excuses nor even explanations for his moves. It is that absolute – unconstrained and unquestionable – decisionist liberty that renders us all, his subjects, dependent on his and only his choices – by definition, unpredictable and on no account manageable by us. As Job learned the hard way: 'this I know for the truth, that no man can win his case against God. If a man chooses to argue with him, God will not answer one question in a thousand' (Job 9: 2–3).

Paradoxically, though, the 'fear and trembling' generated – as Kierkegaard would say – by confrontation with such an absolute, overbearing and overpowering, inscrutable and incalculable might happens to be an ingenious and effective cultural stratagem capable of rendering endurable – indeed, liveable – a life lived in the face of a stubbornly impenetrable fate. Instead of exacerbating, it mitigates the otherwise incurable terrors of the unknown. God, Father, the King sees farther and hears more than I do; not only does he know what the future has in store, but makes it pliable – being able to change its course at will. He is omniscient and omnipotent; if he desists from doing what I would dearly wish to be done, it must be because he knows what I, with my inferior antennae and reason, don't know and wouldn't comprehend if I knew – for instance, that doing it would have brought more evil than good. After all, there is no step he would be unable to take if so he decided. Awareness of his omniscience and omnipotence is reassuring: it may result in a in-him-I-trust self-confidence – all the more so as the decisionist prerogatives of God–Father–Sovereign used to come in a package deal, supplemented by detailed instructions how to ingratiate oneself in his eyes and earn his benevolence and grace while avoiding his wrath. All in all, God–Father–Sovereign are the warrants of the world's order and justice (at least of the part of the world made especially relevant by my presence in it), which can be neither wished nor argued away and which are in no way harmed by my incomprehension, insufficient knowledge, or indeed ignorance or disbelief.

I tend to pick up 1755 as the year in which the warrant for the eviction of God from the centre of the Universe began to be drafted – though, rather than speaking of eviction, those who sketched it preferred to speak of the dereliction of duty by the current resident of the Centre, or of the elopement of an insolvent lodger. In 1755, a triple disaster – earthquake, fire and flood in rapid succession – befell Lisbon, at that time generally viewed as one of the principal centres of European power, wealth, trade, knowledge and arts. Lisbon was destroyed, but blows were falling at random: as Voltaire was quick to observe, 'l'innocent, ainsi que le coupable / soubit également ce mal inevitable' ('the innocent, as much as the guilty, equally suffer that evil inescapable'). Voltaire's verdict was crystal clear: God's sojourn in the centre of the Universe failed to pass the test of reason and morality set by humans; and so did the recommendations of his earthly plenipotentiaries as to the ways of promoting and making binding the criteria which reason and morality would recommend. Implied by that verdict was the resolution that the Universe would have every chance of a better – 'civilized' – order, and more justice, once taken under a new – human – management.

Over the two centuries that followed, we have learned, however – and the hard way – that human managers don't fall far behind God when it comes to the capacity of wreaking havoc with rationality and moral sense – just as we've learned the Great Unknown's resistance to stepping back, and the steadfastness of constraints that stop human managers well short of reaching omniscience, let alone omnipotence. State and market, the two agencies that reason and morality devised – in mutual consultation, though not necessarily full agreement – as the agencies hoped either to properly manage the man-inhabited part of the Universe or to enable the self-same part of the Universe to properly self-manage failed and continue to fail successive practical tests on an all but growing number of occasions, frustrating the expectations invested in them. And there are no obvious candidates in sight so far ready to replace them in the assigned role – however zealous and desperate are the searches, and however much the drawing-board sketches are imaginative and deemed attractive.

In our fractal reality, a similar conundrum repeats itself – even if on a changed scale – on every level of societal organization. The crisis of authority modelled on the image of the omniscient and omnipotent God Father is acutely felt from top to bottom – even if each level has its own reasons to experience it as such, as well as a distinct set of factors responsible for this experience. You have surely noted the recent rediscovery and fast-rising popularity of Blaise Pascal's musing on the nature of the Universe and our, humans', casting in it: 'This is an infinite sphere, the center of which is everywhere, but its circumference nowhere. In short, it is one of the greatest sensible evidences of the almightiness of God, that our imagination is overwhelmed by these reflections.'[14] A musing strikingly poignant and intimately resonant with our present mood – now, in our times of poly-centric uncertainty, even more than before. What for Pascal could be an 'in God we trust' sort of reassurance-*cum*-consolation tends to sound to our ears like an empty promise.

The fleshy, non-metaphoric father belongs to the

---

smallest fractal in the succession/hierarchy of fractals; he can be seen through a privileged fractal all the same, for staying closest to a direct and daily empirical scrutiny. He is able for that reason to supply the yarn of which visions of more distant and abstract fractals can be, and are, woven. That father comes nearest to the role of a joint – or more correctly the transfer/exchange interface – between the two coexisting, intertwined and interacting modes of human togetherness, distinguished by Victor Turner under the names of *societas* and *communitas*. The trials and tribulation currently afflicting that particular 'Father figure' reflect, in a condensed form, the processes affecting all and any of its extensions and idealizations, on whichever level of the fractal structure they are located. In view of the growing numbers of children growing up in one-parent households, most to the point in the current reflection is perhaps the father figure becoming conspicuous – not unlike Thomas Aquinas' *Deus otiosus* or *absconditus* – mostly through his absence and non-interference. Whether both biological parents stay under one roof or not, the parents–children bonds are increasingly loose, simultaneously stripped of their near-identification overlap with the structure of authority. And considering the cognitive privilege of the smallest (and so most commonly accessible to scrutiny) fractal, no wonder that the experience derived from it serves as a matrix – whereas other father figures, specific to other, larger fractals, can be seen as so many permutations it permits and renders probable.

On a number of occasions (most recently in a Spanish book, *El retorno del péndulo* – 'Return of the Pendulum', 2015 – written with Gustavo Dessal) I compared the roles of (by now bygone) 'masturbation panic' and (presently gathering in force) 'child-abuse panic'. The first panic located the be-wary-of danger in torpid and treacherous child sexuality, laying thereby grounds for parental strict, obtrusive and ubiquitous surveillance and control over children's conduct. The second also views children's bedrooms and bathrooms as natural dens of vice, but in its case it is the parents' sexuality – and in particular its presumed paedophile edge – that stands accused, commanding thereby parents to keep their distance and hold under strict control their (now endemically suspicious) intimacy reflexes. Parents are thus drawn away from much of the – previously assumed as self-evident and highly commended – parental calling.

For those reasons, I believe Lacan's and Recalcati's 'evaporation of the father' from family life, or at any rate from that 'centre to which family life gravitates', to be to a large extent – though, of course, not exclusively – a self-inflicted and Do-It-Yourself predicament. It is true that the volatility of the labour markets and the inbuilt frailty, friability, and all-in-all the endemic non-finality of social standings disclose daily the spectacular absence of omniscience, not to mention omnipotence, from the list of the Father's qualities – those new life realities sap the socially produced and maintained conditions on which the possibility to deploy the Family Father as the prototype of all and any future warrants of the world's order and justice used to rest. Yet the Father's 'evaporation', as well as its most seminal *Weltanschauung* consequences like the sudden emptying of 'the gravitation centre', have been aided and abetted by the enforced or voluntary, resigned or enthusiastic, surrender of a large part of parental responsibilities.

And let me add that the moral scruples that might eventually follow such surrender tend to be tackled with purchasable services on the consumer market – and most commonly by the use of the goods they offer in the capacity of, so to speak, moral tranquillizers. This in turn opens the gate ever wider to the commercialization of the most intimate aspects of human togetherness and interaction.

5

Literature and the Interregnum

Riccardo Mazzeo   Adolfo Fattori establishes a parallelism between the disorientation felt by individuals at the transition between the nineteenth and twentieth centuries (quoting Werfel, 'Belonging to two worlds, embracing two ages with a single soul, a truly paradoxical condition, which rarely repeats itself in history and is imposed on but few human generations')[1] and the same disorientation we feel a century later in the interregnum you spoke about, where, as Antonio Gramsci foresaw, the old ways of living in the world no longer work but new ways have yet to be invented. What can literature tell us about this?

Robert Walser, a real favourite of Coetzee, pre-empts the contemporary nomad of liquid modernity. The difference between Walser and the contemporary *déraciné* is the former's total lack of plans, his choice of the trivial, the safe, the insignificant, while the contemporary traveller instead finds himself always having to chase after short-term projects, and, instead of walking like Walser, who made slow and never-ending journeys on foot for hundreds of kilometres, has to hurtle on like an ice-skater in order not to fall and risk not being able to get up again. Moreover, the condition of extreme poverty, of fragmentation and of humiliation, which for Walser was his *own* choice, becomes for his modern follower *another person's* choice, a consequence of the insecurity which 'governs' today's world. Lastly, Walser's eagerness to withdraw and shield himself, to disappear to the point of being shut up in a mental home, counters contemporary man's desire to be visible at any cost, and the sentence that instead condemns him, lacking resources in a scenario of ever-rising poverty, to marginalization, exclusion and being ostracized from the table of the well-to-do. In your opinion, what are the similarities between the two *fins de siècle*?

Zygmunt Bauman Werfel's/Fattori's sentiment of 'Belonging to two worlds, embracing two ages', that shocking experience that the horrors of a four-year-long trench war visited, at the threshold of the twentieth century, without warning, upon the totally unprepared descendants/alumni of the rambunctious, self-confident and self-conceited nineteenth: is it parallel to the state of our minds and our hearts in this age of interregnum? It is not. All similarities, as Hollywood legal disclaimers used to insist, are purely (well, perhaps mostly) coincidental.

Two worlds, two ages? Were there but two worlds to confront, to link or to separate, oppose or reconcile – would we notice that at all? We, who from early childhood and throughout our lives are forced/cajoled to navigate between so many – coinciding and clashing, or following each other in rapid succession? Far from shocking, the sensation of being drawn abruptly and brutally into the new world(s), as well as of being baffled and confused by unseen sights and un-thought thoughts, are for us the comforting signs of normality, of things being on the right (at any rate, familiar) track.

Need to be born again – aren't we practising this daily? Trivially humdrum is the very opposite of shocking. Starting from scratch? And where else could new years or days start? Novelty – unanticipated and unexpected novelties? Yes, we know, they are aplenty – there is hardly anything more familiar nowadays than unfamiliarity, and more ordinary than extraordinariness. What is no longer familiar, though – and, frankly speaking, difficult to comprehend – is the mystery aura and near-eschatological status surrounding novelty – that by now fully and truly repetitive, routine occurrence of reincarnation, being born again, entering a new world, facing the need to embrace the heretofore un-embraceable.

Robert Walser: huge thanks to you, Riccardo, for inviting him to join in our conversation. Walser, not just a favourite of Coetzee, but a 'constant companion' for W. G. Sebald and the 'essential writer of our time' for Elias Canetti. It was opined by Herman Hesse that 'if he [Walser] had a hundred thousand readers, the world would be a better place' (alas he had not, and the world is not). Attempting to locate Walser in the history of modern art, Susan Sontag assigned to him a role akin to that played by a railway junction or transshipment quay: 'a Paul Klee in prose – as delicate, as sly, as haunted', a 'good-humoured, sweet Beckett', 'the missing link between Kleist and Kafka' – so she opines, recalling that Robert Musil, when discovering Kafka, described his discovery as 'a peculiar case of the

Walser type').[2] No doubt, he is a crucial figure in the modern arts' brief yet stormy, and occasionally heroic, story – though, by the verdict of fate, one arguably most remarkable among the unsung and thus poorly recognizable heroes of that story. Allow me, for that reason, to stay with him for a bit longer and try to explain the need for doing so at a length a bit greater than it would otherwise need to be.

Walser was a poet of the anti-heroic, of the limited, the humbled and the small (though perhaps not 'insignificant'!). The daily, the mundane, the taken for granted to the point of invisibility was to him – I suppose – the sole significance of life. In 'The Walk' (the longest of his hundreds of short stories), Walser makes what amounts to his declaration of faith:

> Without walking and the contemplation of nature which is connected with it, without this equally delicious and admonishing search, I deem myself lost, and I am lost. With the utmost love and attention the man who walks must study and observe every smallest living thing, be it a child, a dog, a fly, a butterfly, a sparrow, a worm, a flower, a man, a house, a tree, a hedge, a snail, a mouse, a cloud, a hill, a leaf, or no more than a poor discarded scrap of paper on which, perhaps, a dear good child at school has written his first clumsy letters. The highest and lowest, the most serious and the most hilarious things are to him equally beloved, beautiful, and valuable.[3]

In the short story 'Nervous', Walser avers: 'Grouches, grouches, one must have them, and one must have the courage to live with them, that's the nicest way to live. Nobody should be afraid of his little bit of weirdness.'[4] Of Kleist, hero of one of his most brilliant short stories,

Walser wrote with unconcealed approval and admiration: 'He finds no majestic music so beautiful, no
soul so subtle as the music and soul of all this human
activity.' What would the alternative to this choice of
importance be like? 'Conduct an idiotic or generally
useful debate with some respected official half-wit or
other? [. . .] One would like to seize a sledgehammer
and beat a way out of it all. Get away there, get away!'[5]
At about the same time Kafka would scribble down in
one of his parables, 'The Departure': '"So you know
your goal?" he asked. "Yes", I replied. "I've just told
you. Out of here – that's my goal".'[6] Not long after,
Samuel Beckett would note: 'I don't know. I'll never
know, in the silence you don't know, you must go on,
I can't go on, I can't go on, I'll go on.' Or, for that
matter, Ionesco: 'I feel that every message of despair is
the statement of a situation from which everyone must
freely try to find a way out.'[7]

As Sontag somewhat quizzically suggests in the
quoted essay, 'Walser's art is the refusal of power: of
domination.' He 'assumes depression and terror in
order (mostly) to accept it – ironize over it, lighten it'.
Well, I ask: rebellion, or armistice? Rejection of domination, or its acceptance? Curiously, both – I guess. Or,
perhaps more correctly – though no less enigmatically –
promoting refusal-through-acceptance. Before going on,
however, we might agree that a final verdict on Walser's
own stand – an interpretation to put an end to all further interpreting – is not on the cards, and heed W. G.
Sebald's argument[8] that, towards the end of his uncannily vitiated life-itinerary, Walser, along with Gogol, his
– in Sebald's opinion – only genuine 'literary relative or
predecessor':

---

gradually lost the ability to keep their eyes on the centre of the plot, losing themselves instead in the almost compulsive contemplation of strangely unreal creations appearing on the periphery of their vision . . . in the end it becomes almost impossible to make out Gogol and Walser among the legions of their characters, not to mention against the dark horizon of their looming illnesses.

Amidst the hubbub of competing interpretations, Sebald throws the towel into the ring: 'Who and what Robert Walser really was is a question to which, despite my strangely close relationship with him, I was unable to give any reliable answer.'

Having heard such confession and nodded understandingly and approvingly at what it announced, most Walser readers engaged in reconstructing the real – the one and only – meaning of Walser's message would find their hopes of ever reaching the conclusion fizzling out. At any rate, the most reasonable among them would.

While keeping in mind the above qualifications, let me return to the thorny issue of Walser's attitude to domination. Throughout *Jakob von Gunten*, acclaimed by many critics as his magnum opus, Walser declares training in taking and holding the stance of 'keeping nice and calm', the most advisable stance for people desiring to master the art of decent/proper demeanour, to be the purpose of joining the 'Benjamenta Institute' in which the action of the novel is located. To acquire this stance and hold to it whatever might happen, mere obedience of rules and desisting from all and any rebellion against the authority that set them are not enough. Obedience must be supplemented by non-complaining – but even meeting that stipulation wouldn't suffice if

one didn't stop minding those 'musts' and didn't grow
to like them – actually, sincerely, wholeheartedly and
without compunction. The Jakob of the title, who
started by staunchly resenting the Benjamenta Institute's
rule of eating up to the last crumb the contents of the
dinner plate one was served, ends up (though not without time-consuming training and an extended, but ever
more easy to perform, self-drilling) by eating 'everything
up as tidily as any of the pupils. I even look forward
every time to the nicely prepared and modest meals.'
Jakob thinks of Elves – growing on him incessantly
as his lodestars – as the ideals he is ever more eager to
emulate; he praises their habit of doing 'all their rough
and laborious tasks out of pure, supernatural goodness
of heart'. Obedience streaming from such a source is no
longer serfdom, but freedom – but it is more than that in
fact: an insurance policy against all future humiliation
and an antidote to all future poisons. Domination may
be invincible and bound to last forever, but a whole-
hearted acceptance of its non-negotiable invincibility
may strip it of its fangs and claws and toxic stings . . .
'I don't note such things anymore', Jakob observes with
self-congratulating aplomb. The 'things' which he notes
no more are the acts of surrender hidden behind the
masks of free choices. Nothing is seen – so nothing pains
and nothing hurts. And the road to this supreme bliss of
un-noticing is straightforward, even if somewhat bumpy
and with stretches uneasy to negotiate: the sole secret is
to desire to do, and to love doing, what you must.

A road. Or more precisely: one of two branches of
the eminently bifurcated road of life. The other branch
is signposted by Albert Camus: 'I rebel, therefore we
exist.' In literature, just as in sociology, it is the roads

to truth that people seek, take or blunder into that are explored, with the truth itself forever outstanding and waiting for a Messiah to lay it bare. But, as Kafka had already, for better or worse, concluded – the Messiah comes a day after his arrival.

It is tempting to choose that Messiah's peculiarity as the definition of the state of 'interregnum'. Or, rather, to accept that a state of interregnum arrives when we feel obliged to invest our hopes in that peculiarity – because our days are filled with seeking, yet void of findings; and that state stays as long as we feel like that.

6

The Blog and the Disappearance of Mediators

Riccardo Mazzeo We have already mentioned Jonathan Franzen during our talks: I appreciated his two main novels, *The Corrections* and *Freedom*; on the other hand, you were aware of some very relevant aspects in his collection of brief essays *Farther Away*, before it was translated into Italian, and I completely agreed with his point of view on the seductive influence of his latest-model BlackBerry and on the destructive potential of the 'facilitation' aspect provided by technology: the novelist who had captivated and moved me then became something more – a person with whom I would have liked to discuss things that exist even outside his narrative work.

Then, almost inevitably, he published his long essay *The Kraus Project*, in which he pays homage to the mediator of his youth and at the same time performs a triple somersault that seems rather like an antidote to today's prevailing trend to facilitate and inevitably flatten everything. He chooses an extremely difficult author – the satirical writer Kraus, to be precise – and quotes his own translation of *Heine and the Consequences* (and other texts by Kraus), disseminating it with a gigantic corpus of footnotes that partly explain the most difficult passages of the text and contextualize it, and that partly trace parallels between the Vienna of a century ago and Western society today. Last of all, he partly speaks of himself, Franzen, and the demolition of previous authors (from John Updike to Philip Roth) – a demolition that he had attempted in his younger years, in the same way (although with far more modest results) that Kraus had slaughtered the author who, together with Goethe, had been the greatest nineteenth-century writer in the German language, and a Jew converted to Catholicism: Heinrich Heine.

The first thing in the book that catches the reader's eye is that the review founded by Kraus in 1899, *Die Fackel* ('The Torch'), was very similar to the blogs that are all the rage today. In addition, between 1911 and 1936, the author wrote all the articles himself and filled them with his creative genius and his venom. The main difference from contemporary blogs is that, while blogs have no following or achieve fleeting success, *Die Fackel* was read by the most eminent figures of the day in Central Europe (Mitteleuropa) including Freud, Kafka, Wittgenstein, Thomas Mann, Adorno and Walter Benjamin; another difference was that Kraus' writing was extremely complex and deliberately cryptic in tone, in order to keep the more commonplace minds at arms' length. In reality, Kraus' 'antiblog' blog constituted an attempt, as fervent as it was desperate, to defend the German language and spirit that had been trivialized by a Heine who was happy only when he was in Paris. I feel that Franzen is just as heroic and passionate in his attempt to defend authentic literature and ideas from the irresistible temptation of the Internet: 'Who has time to read literature when there are so many blogs to keep up with, so many food fights to follow on Twitter?'[1]

Basically, both Kraus ('Art brings disorder in life. The poets of humanity continue to repeat chaos')[2] and Franzen invite the reader to tear the mind-numbing veil of the vulgate to try to penetrate reality, which is quite different from the reassuring screen that we insist on being glued to. It reminds me of one of the questions that you were asked by Tester and Jacobsen in *What Use Is Sociology?*,[3] on the responsibilities attributable to kindness compared to the status quo, to which you replied that, if anything, kindness is conspicuous for its disheartening absence. *Prudence*, and even *cowardice*, determined by a cautious and fearful attitude shaped more by the act of survival than by life and living, attempts to safeguard us from the unpleasant consequences of our actions but should not be confused with the genuine kindness that is shown by a friendly manner towards the other person, considered as a kindred being, like a brother. In his two latest books,[4] Eugenio Borgna speaks of the strong need for kindness towards others – who, because they are human, are congenitally affected by that fragility common to us all – and especially the sick, the elderly, the poor and the excluded. This is totally different from the concept of the *hypocrisy* of those who are afraid to make enemies, of those who choose the *politically correct* option and end up, like many writers, by turning aside from their own personal mission. After discussing the difficulties that writers encounter today in making a living from their work, Franzen adds:

Nevertheless, what saddens me is that at a time when a relatively low percentage of the New York literary scene manages to make a living by writing, a high percentage of this scene is so prudent. [. . .] Woe betide any female writer who is a bit tough with her characters. Far more than in the past, this harshness would be a sufficient reason for a (prudently) negative critique. [. . .] harsh criticism of the electronic system that makes writers so soporific signifies running the risk of being labelled by public opinion as a hater, as antisocial, not *one of us.*[5]

It is also true that there are thousands of critical blogs, and vitriol belongs to the young who have a healthy evolutionary need of 'all or nothing', of dichotomous categories to be blurred later when they have grown up. In his late teenage years, Franzen himself was struck by an explosive Kraus, 'almost like a rapper', who wrote of 'intellectual work of the virility that forges language [. . .] that will be differentiated from the craft of easy learning of linguistic kindness', and admits thirty years later to having been 'blissfully ignorant of the dangerous territory Kraus entered by speaking of the "flood of filth unleashed by the Jew Heine"'.[6] But if the cycles of life are to be respected today, compared to this often blind vehemence (which may be desirable at twenty, but is unacceptable at fifty) the fundamental difference is revealed in the somewhat excessive calibre of Kraus, compared to the mercurial superficiality of the positions that are generally assumed these days. Moreover, 100 years before, Kraus had grasped how much damage could be inflicted on the imagination by the small-minded press; by the lifestyle journalism that emotionally pre-masticated news and images for the reader, as in TV programmes today; poetry ready to be set to music – however beautiful – like that written by Heine; and so many novels written like a screenplay – already aimed at the income to be gained from the movie adaptation.

So the problem does not lie so much with how much you do or what you sing when you are twenty; at that age, Franzen himself was singing the refrain by Richard Hell, the punk poet-singer and ex-husband of Patti Smith, who foresaw social networking ('I belong to the blank generation and I can take it or leave it each time').[7]

In conclusion, *The Kraus Project* is completely focused on the loss of mediators, on the increasing rarity of that miracle that is essential to the continuation of culture and life: *transmission.* Franzen had received from his German professor George (his surname was also Kraus!) a book by Karl Kraus as a wedding gift. George had been like a second father to him, he had taught him about the deep relationship that exists between literature and life, and for this reason Franzen decided to translate the impenetrable texts of Karl Kraus.

In my own little corner of the world – which is to say, American fiction – Jeff Bezos of Amazon may not be the anti-Christ, but he surely looks like one of the four horsemen. Amazon wants a world in which books are either self-published or published by Amazon itself, with readers dependent on Amazon reviews in choosing books, and with authors responsible for their own promotion. The work of yakkers and tweeters and braggers, and of people with the money to pay somebody to churn out hundreds of five-star reviews for them, will flourish in that world. [. . .] But what will happen to those who become a writer *precisely because* yakking, twittering and bragging seemed to be a form of intolerably superficial social interaction?[8]

Transmission *is not* in any way a cloning; thanks to transmission, if all goes well, one becomes what one was destined to become – in other words, something different. However, it is essential in order to access oneself. How can we become our true selves without a heritage, without a guide, without their voice, without a significant message?

Zygmunt Bauman A universally binding law whose articulation is credited sometimes to Thomas Gresham and some other times to Nicolaus Copernicus, but whose early formulation could be found as much as two millennia earlier in Aristophanes' *Frogs*, says, in the nutshell, that 'bad money drives out good money'. In times knowing of no other money than gold, silver or copper coins, 'bad' money meant coins stopping short of their promise: coins whose metal was worth less than their nominal value. When such coins appeared in circulation, the 'good' among them tended to disappear from common use (locked, as it were, in the vaults of a relatively few exceptionally circumspect and lucky – or just greedy – hoarders).

That law, however, has much wider application than its wording suggests. Coins are, after all, means of exchange, and if there are less costly means that you can use to obtain what you are after, why should you give away those more valuable? In the case of the bad vs good money, the mechanism operating the Gresham/Copernicus Law is set in motion and driven by pecuniary greed; in other cases, however, it may be (and it is) set in motion by other factors – for instance, by a desire for greater comfort, coupled with a distaste for inconvenience. This is, in fact, a powerful motive – and it links the Gresham/Copernicus Law to the issue which you raise, taking a leaf from Jonathan Franzen: the predicament of 'language in the blog-and-twitter land' – and, through language, that principal medium of communicative exchange, also to the issue of the fate/destiny of our powers of expression and comprehension.

Alas, I haven't read either Franzen's *The Kraus Project* (copies of which are promised to be available, unfortunately, only later in the year), or Karl Kraus's anti-Heine pamphlet – and can't therefore respond to your quandary point by point. But knowing Franzen's other writings – and also, I believe, the cause for which he carries the banner – I feel capable of engaging with the gist of your (and my!) worry. And the gist of our shared worry is the impact of the new electronic media (an impact not yet fully known, and for that reason suggestive of yet more worries to come) on who we are, on what we do to each other, and how we live with each other. Franzen has an exceedingly sharp eye on the influences of new electronic media upon our behaviour, worldview and expectations: both their salient influences (for instance, the veritable 'national orgy of connectedness': enabling and encouraging invasion of personal and individual matters into the public and communal – which constitutes 'the very essence of the cell phone's hideousness'),[9] and influences not so obvious, though no less damaging (for instance, aiding and abetting our misleading and corrupting solecisms as the 'fantasy ideal of erotic relationship').[10]

What is that 'fantasy ideal' like, however? Franzen starts from confessing that, having disposed of a three-year-old BlackBerry Pearl and exchanged it for a brand new BlackBerry Bold, he 'wanted to keep fondling' his new toy. He 'was, in short, infatuated with [his] new device'. But this is precisely what we feel about, and how we behave towards, an object of erotic exaltation, isn't it? Or rather what we would do and feel, were that 'object' not also a subject – that is, an entity complete with desires, preferences, priorities and will all of its own, and of a kind that may, but also may not, agree with ours. 'Real-life' objects of erotic ecstasy stop well short of the ideal to which the BlackBerry Bold came so close! The ideal of erotic raptures, unlike their human objects, 'asks for nothing and gives everything, instantly' – with no procrastination or as much as a murmur of protest or the vaguest gesture of displeasure. It is, in the language of commercials, 'user friendly' (read: fully and truly 'user obedient'). Yet, perhaps more importantly, it 'does not throw terrible scenes when it's replaced by an even sexier object and is consigned to a drawer'. Did you hear BlackBerry Pearl sobbing its heart out, or swearing/cursing, on the way to the dustbin?! You didn't, that is for sure. No one did. So why could John or Mary not behave more like that BlackBerry Pearl when its moment of departure arrived? John or Mary should have been aware from the start, and accept, that their capability of giving 'everything' – that is, every pleasure which one can conceivably hope for in the absence of 'sexier objects' – surely won't survive the appearance of the latter?!

This so-called 'progress' – 'marching forward', whether singly, severally or all together – leads (by the explicitly articulated or tacitly presumed definition of 'forward') from less comfort/convenience to more; and from more inconvenience/trouble/bother to less. The trajectory of 'progress' is marked by more results achieved at lesser cost and effort, and results achieved quicker than before when counting the time needed to produce the desired result as well as the time needed to acquire the skills to do it. In the world containing matches and lighters, we are utterly unlikely to return to the use of flint and tinder – if not for any other reason, then for having been given enough time to comfortably forget the skills necessary to make them work.

The issue you raise of the widely welcome (*sic*!) chance to simplify/vulgarize the language, which not so long ago we needed to swot hard and interminably to master in all its cryptic complexity of grammar, syntax and orthography – the chance brought about by the 'messaging' and 'twittering' appliances and the standards and routines that follow their introduction – is a similar case. Why bend over backward to attain what can be had with little or no effort? Why wait endlessly for results that could be instantaneous? And just try to consider that most complex business of them all, that most risky and demanding – yet, all the same, the least avoidable – life-business of falling, and even more staying, in love?!

There are numerous and quite serious reasons to expect that 'progress' in that most intricate and complex field of life occurrences, currently offered by and in the 'online' part of the human universe, will be capable of perpetrating direct and 'collateral' damages more profound, lasting and seminal than in any other area or aspect of the human mode of being-in-the-world-inhabited-by-humans. While any gain tends to be accompanied by some losses (as folk wisdom plaintively, albeit rightly, opines: 'you win some, you lose some'), the loss of precisely those qualities of love from which we are, so temptingly, promised liberation in the online safety zone portends to be fully and truly irreparable and devastating in its consequences. Love is happiness – but being in love is also an ongoing lesson that happiness hardly ever comes ready for instant consumption and insured against pain; and that, far from being the antonym of happiness, the pain and the hard job of conquering it happen to be also the *sine-qua-non* ingredients of the very stuff out of which love relations are built. Painless love is a lie and a hoax; an equivalent of alcohol-free beer or calorie-free food or, for that matter, pennies from heaven. But if love is not a recipe for (let alone a guarantee of) happiness, the absence of love renders happiness all but a foreign country: *terra incognita*, as a matter of fact.

Let me quote Franzen one last time. Referring again to his own – marital, this time – experience, he observes:

> our struggle to honor our commitments actively came to constitute who we were as people; we were not helium molecules, floating inertly through life; we bonded and we changed. For another thing [. . .] pain hurts, but it doesn't kill. When you consider the alternative – an anaesthetized dream of self-sufficiency, abetted by technology – pain emerges as the natural product and natural indicator of being alive in a resistant world. To go through a life painlessly is not to have lived. Even just to say to yourself, 'Oh, I'll get to that love and pain stuff later, maybe in

my thirties', is to consign yourself to ten years of merely taking up space and burning up its resources [spoken, let us note, to the alumni of a college during a commencement ceremony].[11]

7
Are We All Becoming Autistic?

Riccardo Mazzeo Recently, in Paris where I spent some time writing a conversation/book with Miguel Benasayag on the situation of the elderly and the upheaval in modern life cycles today, I met the philosopher Jean-Michel Besnier, who teaches at the Sorbonne and who took part in the first meeting at Miguel's home. Given the excellent first impression he made on me, I immediately read his latest book, *L'Homme simplifié: la syndrome de la touche étoile* ('The Simplified Man'),[1] and I have noted a few points that are perhaps relevant to the topic we are discussing.

Besnier's theory agrees with that expressed by Adorno in *Minima Moralia: Reflections From Damaged Life*: 'Behind the apparent clarity and transparency in human relationships where nothing undefined is tolerated, pure brutality is unleashed.'[2] There is no doubt that delegating to technology and quantification makes life simpler and more clearly defined, but at the same time we sacrifice the nuances, the ups and downs, the contradictions and the complexities that make human beings . . . well – human.

In the previous chapter, I spoke to you about the disappearance of mediators, those sources from whom we drink to develop and become ourselves. Hierarchies of the past could present weaknesses/flaws depending on the influence of the logic of the times, but the 'great writers' still showed certain elements of greatness: you could go to a bookshop or a library to fill up on accredited knowledge.

Moreover, back then you could chat to your bookseller, you would accept his advice; there was a real person with a passion for books with whom you could compare notes in order to make a careful choice of the books to take home. However, today, the independent book-sellers (the true, authentic kind) are being forced to close, one after another crushed by the large distribution chains that are very efficiently computerized, but just as efficiently dehumanized, and our children seek their knowledge on the Internet. But Besnier states: 'When we discover that Google sells to the highest bidder those key words that permit the selection and hierarchization of research results, we become aware of the true danger that looms over the acculturation and absorption of knowledge that information and communications technology maintains it wishes to facilitate.'[3]

Besnier refers back to Descartes to identify the warning signs of a development of scientific thought based on simplification and the refusal of the inexpressible, but also recalls the Orwellian dystopia of *1984* in which Newspeak managed to delete the 'redundant shades of meaning' present in Oldspeak and to transform the words, preserving only their root meaning and freeing them from the semantic complications of their reality. When their density is eliminated, words become 'operations' and are left at the mercy of manipulation by the dominant. On the other hand, while kids reduce their text words to their lowest denomination, there is a proliferation of abbreviations and acronyms that is rapidly demolishing the dignity and true meaning of our language: 'When the Healthcare System becomes SSN, or the old Health Service is called ASL, it is probable that personal relations with any kind of social benefits or social security under collective management have disappeared.'[4]

I also liked Besnier's book because, as well as quoting the interview/book that you wrote with Benedetto Vecchi and your *Life in Fragments* (1993), underlining the association of complication with the 'solid' world and simplification with the 'liquid' world, he also quotes Gunther Anders – who, as you recalled in *A Natural History of Evil* (2012), spoke of the envy of machinery that man has developed – and Alain Ehrenberg, whom you referred to in *44 Letters* (2010), in relation to the transition, common in psychotherapy patients, in moving from a sense of guilt to a sense of helplessness. I think the incapacity to feel a sense of guilt was shown in a truly excellent way in Haneke's film *Caché* (2005), in which Georges (Daniel Auteuil), a well-cultured and wealthy television host, lives in a beautiful house where the countless books lining the walls and framing the large TV seem to form a fortress to protect him and his lovely wife Anne (Juliette Binoche) from the 'ordinary' world. Despite being surrounded by amusing, intelligent friends, signs of cracks in the wall seem to come from the twelve-year-old son with whom Georges and Anne have no form of communication, but the secret of a shameful event from Georges' past life gradually emerges after the arrival of unmarked videotapes left on their doorstep together with a crayon drawing of a bleeding child.

These 'invasions', whose source is never revealed, force Georges to return to his past and reflect on Majid, the son of the Algerian couple who had worked for his family. Georges' parents had decided to adopt Majid after his parents were killed during the protest in Paris against the Algerian war, along with 200 other Algerian protesters. Georges' parents felt a sense of guilt, but Georges, only six years old, used a ploy to get rid of the other child he did not want, who was sent away to an orphanage. Georges manages to trace Majid, who is also a father now; he lives in poor conditions and denies having sent the videotapes and the drawings and, finally, he invites Georges to his home where he slashes his own throat in front of him. Despite the tragedy, even now, Georges feels no sense of guilt.

The salient point is that, in order to feel a sense of guilt in relation to another person, the other must exist as a real person in our eyes, as somebody who 'resonates through us', but in the format of a world where others are perceived as mere instruments or objects to be used to achieve a personal micro- or macro-managerial project, where evaluation is always objective and controllable, success smiles only on those who do not waste time with things like real life – burdened but also enriched by all of life's complexities.

I have always been fascinated by the mystery of autism and have spoken with one of the most talented and famous autistic people in the world (suffering from

Asperger Syndrome): Temple Grandin. My Italian publisher Erickson translated two of her books. I have close tender feelings for people suffering from autism and their special and isolated way of life. But a tendency towards the inaccessibility typical of the autistic spectrum is becoming increasingly more pronounced among the general public and Besnier states that the number of autistic people has increased from 1 person in 5,000, in 1975, to 1 in 110 in 2009.

A fifty-fold increase cannot simply be the result of a more sophisticated ability to identify communication disorders. Many experts evoke 'hypotheses that involve combined environmental factors and genetic traits'.[5] In this case, there would be nothing strange in analysing in a different manner the intensive practice of communicating via email, Twitter or blog, at which autistic people excel and in which we are all becoming engulfed.

So, can it be true that we are all becoming autistic?

Zygmunt Bauman There is not much new under the Sun. A long time ago, Sigmund Freud questioned and all but wiped out the highly contentious borderline between the 'normal' and the 'pathological' in human behaviour and human interaction, together with the barrier separating them from each other – a barrier cemented mostly with conventions seeking simplicity, as well as an 'either-or' kind of un-ambiguity, in what is in fact an incurably, irreducibly complex *Lebenswelt*. The profusion of qualifications, circumscriptions, provisos and riders accompanying any attempted definition of 'autism', and the tentative status of any list of its symptoms, leave little doubt as to the 'essentially contested'

– as well as indecisive, indeed vague – standing of the concept. You'd find on the official website of 'Autistica', an institution describing itself as engaged in a 'pioneering medical research to understand the causes of autism, improve diagnosis, and develop new treatments and interventions', that 'We are the UK's leading autism medical research charity, and we are committed to funding translational research that will make a difference to people's lives.' Having established its credentials in the above way, Autistica proceeds to spell out the convoluted nature of the condition at the centre of its attention: 'The autism spectrum is very broad. Some people have no language, intellectual difficulties and cannot engage with others. Other people on the autism spectrum (such as those with Asperger Syndrome) may have very good or even advanced language skills but find the rules governing social behaviour hard to fathom.'[6] Equally frequent are the phrases expressing indecision as to the causes of the ailments under discussion:

> The environmental factors that play a role in autism are more challenging to reliably identify. It is also unclear how these environmental factors may interact with a person's genetic risk for developing autism. Research has not yet identified a direct causal link between any environmental factor and autism (including vaccinations), although risk for developing autism has been associated with factors such as parental age.

Most confused and confusing are perhaps the suggested symptoms of autism: most frequently named are difficulty with social communication, difficulty with social interaction and difficulty with social imagination.[7] But don't we all experience, at one time or another – and not all that seldom – such types of difficulty? Given the commonality of experience, the estimate of half a million Britons suffering acute or mild forms of 'autism' feels uncannily like a shot in the dark.

'[C]an it be true that we are all becoming autistic?', you ask, and you have all sorts of good reasons to do so, considering that the difficulty with 'sociality' – with an interaction aimed at mutual understanding, and at thrashing out by shared effort the obstacles standing in the way of that purpose (which is thus an activity gaining in importance, day in, day out, as diasporization of the planet goes on resulting in an increasing variegation, heterogeneity and multi-centred nature of habitats) – is one of the most common and insidious afflictions harrowing our contemporaries and bound to do so for a long time to come.

'Sociality', we may say, is a stance and a practice of curiosity: of keeping the gate open to risky adventures as-yet-unexplored and disturbingly unknown. It is an attitude of toning down, and better still suppressing, the impulse of withdrawal from communication – of separation, fencing off and locking the doors. What sociality enables is a take-off to Hans Maria Gadamer's 'fusion of horizons' – but more is needed to pave the way to 'joining forces': that is, to solidarity, a Siamese twin of cooperation. Somewhere on the road leading from sociality to solidarity, acquisition of new skills must happen: crucial skills of sharing the world and interacting with difference – the skills without which overcoming the dread of the 'strange', obscure and thus far inscrutable – and all too often the demobilizing and potentially paralysing unease/consternation experienced in the face of uncertainty (that is, ignorance how to proceed) – is impossible. The trouble is, though, that numerous aspects of present-day society tend to bar acquisition of such skills, or tempt us to avoid the hard labour of their acquisition. They do it in subtle or crude ways, openly (through 'appealing-to-reason' recommendations explicitly given) or surreptitiously (through manipulating the settings of interaction and the tools of acting). Online shelter from the discomforting diversity of offline existence is one of the major ways – perhaps the major and most effective – in which such inopportune effects may be engendered.

It seems that the empire that has by now invaded, annexed and colonized roughly a half of our waking lives – the 'online' empire – currently sets the tune which more and more of us willingly join in to hum. Its impact on the popular (indeed increasingly common and ever more likely to become universal) *savoir-être* and *savoir-faire* is expanding and deepening day in, day out. The online half of the dual universe we inhabit offers the possibility of sweeping under the carpet the challenges of cohabitation with diversity – a kind of possibility almost inconceivable in the offline world: in a school, workplace, neighbourhood, city street. Instead of facing up to such challenges point-blank and embarking on the long, bumpy and tortuous road leading from sociality to cooperation and from cooperation to solidarity, it tempts its visitors with an elsewhere unattainable luxury of fencing them off, rendering them irrelevant and ignoring them. What it offers as a result is a sort of a 'comfort zone': a stranger-free – and thus trouble-free – area cut out from the hurly-burly of offline realities.

Facebook's 'networks of friends' are digital equivalents of massively corporeal gated communities

– though unlike those offline replicas, they don't need CCTV and armed guards at the entry: the fingers of the network's composer/manager/consumer, armed with a mouse and the magic 'delete' key, are sufficient. The endemic sociality of humans is thereby cleansed of the risk of sidestepping into the treacherous practice of collaboration and the 'fusion of horizons' with which such practice is pregnant – and of morphing, eventually, into solidarity. Without accepting that risk, social skills fall, however, into disuse, and so eventually into oblivion – and as they do, the presence of the stranger grows yet more awesome, off-putting, repelling and horrifying, while the hardships involved in an attempt to elaborate a satisfactory *modus vivendi* with that presence seem all the more overwhelming and, indeed, insurmountable.

Kurt Lewin, the German-American psychologist considered by many a father of social psychology, was commissioned during World War II to attend to front-line soldiers with a rare and at that time undiagnosed disability. While they were able flawlessly to follow rigid, repetitive and uninfringeable routines, the soldiers in question used to fall into a stupor – hapless and helpless – whenever they found themselves in a context requiring a choice between alternative moves. To grasp the nature of their disability, Lewin split the concept of 'action' into two: action on a 'concrete' and on an 'abstract' level – suggesting that the specific ailment of the victims of the front-line contusion was the loss of the ability to act on the second of the two levels. Of great relevance to our issue, I suggest, is the kind of therapy which Lewin designed to deal with the affliction: a living space so planned that its residents never found themselves facing a need to compare, calculate, choose between different options (e.g., one door only in every room, one electrical switch, lines drawn on floors in a particular colour leading to one – and one only – destination). And, indeed, no outside visitor to such a simplified space of *Eindeutigkeit* ('un-ambiguity') was able to perceive any kind of 'abnormality' or pathology in the residents' conduct – that is, until those residents left the compound to join the world that demands the capability to act, intermittently, on both levels.

I wonder . . . aren't the 'social websites' something akin to Kurt Lewin's ingenious contraption – even if the afflictions they are meant to tackle are different? In both cases, we find the same expedient: providing a 'comfort zone' for individuals who feel uncomfortable and at a loss in the 'real world' crowded with incalculable risks, which sets standards for social skills that they are unable, unwilling or not caring enough to meet? A trouble-free zone, a safety zone, a zone inside which one can conduct 'normal life', follow one's desires, gratify one's needs and fulfil one's dreams, without paying the price one would be required to pay if one wished to do all that offline, and without the skills one would need to learn and deploy. Isn't it likely that, as in the case of Lewin's patients, such an expedient won't cure the afflicted of their affliction – if anything, it will allow it to entrench and endure, through mitigating the pressures likely to lay bare its gravity, so stripping the need for a cure of its import and urgency? Won't it be able to achieve that effect through transmogrifying an abnormality into the norm, rendering thereby alternative patterns of interaction yet more off-putting, yet more anxiety-generating, and all in all yet more unlikely to be embraced? And, by the way, making the sufferers of the online-born variety of autism even less fit to operate in the offline world – the world that casts the autistic mode of being-in-the-world as pathological – and so even more dependent on being sheltered inside the online 'safety zone'?

8

Metaphors of the Twenty-first Century

Riccardo Mazzeo   In *What Use Is Sociology?*, I rediscovered an echo of the defence of the metaphor made
by Marcel Proust (the first of my mediators) in *In the
Shadow of Young Girls in Bloom* when speaking of
Elstir. Recalling the fundamental problem of transmission which we discussed earlier, it is significant that
this echo appears in a quotation from a text by your
daughter Anna Sfard:

> Language is as much a part of concept-making as sounds
> are a part of making music. Rather than being viewed as
> a mere instrument for capturing ready-made ideas, it is
> [. . .] the medium within which the creation of new con-
> cepts takes place. It is a bearer of conceptual structures
> we use to organize our experience. [. . .] Thanks to the
> transplants of conceptual structures, language itself is in a
> process of constant development. Like a living organism,
> it has the inevitability of change and growth inscribed in
> its genes. To sum up, one of the most important mes-
> sages of the contemporary research on metaphors is that

language, perception, and knowledge are inextricably intertwined.[1]

More than any other author, Proust used the metaphor in searching for those words that would have been able, and would have known how, to express the ineffable and the discontinuity of the heart that define human beings behind their social masks; he was initially laughed at by the French literary intelligentsia, and especially by Gide, who would later recognize his greatness. But the point lies precisely in Anna Sfard's admirable synthesis, 'language, perception, and knowledge are inextricably intertwined'.

And you explain in your book how the ancients were mistaken in their opinion that metaphors were 'mere adornments of speech, as trinkets one would rather do without for the sake of clarity'.[2] On the contrary, 'metaphors render an enormously important service. They serve imagination and comprehension. They are the indispensable scaffoldings for imagination and perhaps the most effective tools of comprehension.'[3] And you also recall our revered Gregory Bateson and his 'tertiary learning situation: the need to reassemble an established conceptual network too dense or rare to capture novel phenomena in a new cognitive frame to make salient their otherwise unnoticeable traits'.[4]

In the final analysis, when reality changes in an important way and when there are no words to capture the new images that appear before our eyes, we do not know how to describe such instances with words that had been adequate till now, so metaphors can come to our aid. This occurred with the metaphors 'power, class, individual group, human relations, social bonds – even society itself',[5] and it happened admirably with your term 'liquid modernity', which has been adopted by everyone, from the President of the European Central Bank, Mario Draghi, to the brilliant and corrosive *Repubblica* journalist Michele Serra. Metaphors help us to find our direction in the world.

So, other than 'liquid modernity', what would be the metaphors of the twenty-first century? My friend Stefano Tani, a literature professor who has taught for nine years in the USA and has now come back to Italy where he has tenure at the University of Verona, has listed three: *screens, Alzheimer's* and *Zombie*.[6] *Screens* refer to looking at oneself, *Alzheimer's* to emptying oneself, and *Zombie* to transforming oneself.

Tani states that the passage from the written page to the screen through which we access the Internet was preceded by the passage from dialogue to the written word: in fact it was Plato, with his rather condescending and suspicious attitude towards the metaphor, who betrayed Socrates by disobeying his request not to put his words in writing. And, of course, Kafka was also betrayed by his friend Max Brod, who did not respect his instructions to burn his works, and who passed on his masterpieces, which would have otherwise been lost – but *this* passage from the written page to the screen of the computer, tablet or iPhone is far more critical. After all, putting one's thoughts in writing offers deeper insight: a person who writes reflects on his thoughts, developing and elaborating on them further. Writing is to deeper reflection what the network is to fleeting superficiality. Tani writes: 'The world of liquid modernity sees in every underwater diver an aspiring suicide, a man wishing to drown and prefers the seagull that skims across the water pecking at what floats on the surface.'[7]

This is the norm in the days of the selfie, which depends on extreme self-centredness and on the fact that, having excluded society, each person finds himself alone with himself, feeling secure only with himself in a world that is described and perceived as increasingly more menacing and hostile – finally the screen becomes comparable to a mirror, representing the most protective extension of oneself. Tani notes how men and women have traditionally used their working tools holding them from behind: 'from the wheelbarrow to the chainsaw and the vacuum cleaner: generally we do not look the object – so to speak – in the eye. But, as thousands of years ago men and women developed reciprocal feelings for each other when they began to couple face to face, likewise today they are developing dependence, if not affection, for their screen devices since, in order to use them, they must necessarily look them in that eye called display'.[8] And in fact the screen does screen or shield, protecting us from interference from other humans who have become, although not exactly enemies, at least potentially destructive.

Today, on 25 June 2014, I began writing again to conclude this small text for you, and in the *Repubblica* I found a piece that corroborates your concept: in your article there, 'La nostra vita da immigrati digitali' ('Our Lives as Digital Immigrants'), you refer to the price we pay for our comfortable/handy life online – 'attention, concentration, patience and the possibility of long-lasting life'. In his book, Tani discusses the second metaphor of the twenty-first century, Alzheimer's disease:

not through consumption (as in tuberculosis) or invasion (as in cancer), but through evasion, the evacuation of the ego from a body bombarded all its life by an amount of information and demands that are extraordinary in their intensity and number in comparison to those faced by previous generations. [. . .] someone suffering from Alzheimer's disease is like a computer that has survived memory loss, becoming a mere container devoid of its function and therefore of its sense – the motherboard is demagnetized, data overlaid in paths no longer programmed flow down to zero. With his hopeless, mutilated, aphasic and amnesic characters, Samuel Beckett was the pioneer dramatist who anticipated this nullifying metaphor of the 21st century.[9]

The other problem is that this 'emptying' procedure is happening today despite the enormous flow of information that is pouring in because, as you emphasized, memory is delegated to electronic devices, and the 'upgraded' person that we believe we are becoming in this way inevitably loses those capacities that are no longer used. As Tani says, quoting McLuhan, every extension is [also] an amputation: 'Any invention or technology is an extension or self-amputation of our physical bodies, and such extension also demands new ratios or new equilibriums among the other organs and extensions of the body.'[10]

You have often spoken about the new waste management industry that has developed until it has involved the whole of Western society. You wrote that, in the same way the news we receive every day has the principal aim of cancelling and making us forget what we have received up till the previous day, we are too busy cancelling spam and unwanted messages that have managed to infiltrate our 'official' mail box to find the time to write any messages that have some true meaning and that are not mere expressions of electronic etiquette. As Tani writes:

> To save one thing, another is cancelled and everything lasts such a short time, in the same way as the time for any other activities has been reduced: vacations, weddings, and work, often limited by short term contracts. [. . .] Everything is second hand, and we are so used to second hand information and images – but in HD – that anything first hand often seems inadequate.[11]

The image of the Zombie stems from the Alzheimer's metaphor. In a world where the body is being constantly trained in work-out gyms and kept 'thin' and 'in shape' through dieting, it ends up forgetting to bear witness to who we are as it should be doing and, on the contrary, slips through our fingers – projected as we are in virtual connection, our minds remain the only human expression that still has any value. By depriving us of this aspect, Alzheimer's transforms us into undead zombies.

Tani uncovers the very strong connection between Alzheimer's and the electronic devices to which we entrust our ego or 'io' in a compelling comment taken from the novel by Lisa Genova, *Still Alice*[12] (it is perhaps not accidental that the first letter 'i' in iPhone is not reserved for the 'I', or 'Io', but for a phone, as if to concede supremacy to the gadget). Alice is a brilliant Harvard psychology professor with a prodigious memory, who is very strong at multitasking – 'she was always doing three things at once and thinking of twelve'[13] – but at age fifty she is struck with a premature form of Alzheimer's and within a few months her whole life falls to pieces.

Her family talks about her disease in front of her as if she were not present, as if she were some object in the room; speaking in public has become impossible; she relies on instructions she programmes into her BlackBerry, since she forgets everything, just as the characters in *One Hundred Years of Solitude*, by Gabriel García Marquez, struck down by the insomnia plague (and loss of memory), relied on notes written on slips of paper until they were no longer able to understand what they had written. Alice also decides to commit suicide when the treatment she is under ceases to have any effect, and these instructions are also entered into her BlackBerry. But, after a difficult day, her husband finds her cell phone in the freezer, irreparably damaged, and this is truly the end: '*How ridiculous, why am I this upset over a dead electronic organizer?* Maybe the death of her organizer symbolized the death of her position at Harvard, and she was mourning the recent loss of her career. That also made sense. But what she felt was an inconsolable grief over the death of the BlackBerry itself.'[14]

In his book, Tani pays wonderful homage to you and your book *Homo consumens* (2007).[15] The author describes the scene from the second film by George A. Romero on zombies, *Dawn of the Dead* (1978). In this movie the zombies, who, like Lazarus, are not completely dead but not truly alive either, feel an irresistible call back to the place they loved more than any other during their lives – the mall – and it is there that they are seen, staggering and gruesome, by some human survivors who are flying overhead in a helicopter. One asks 'What are they doing? Why do they come here?', and the other answers: 'Some kind of instinct. Memory of what they used to do. This was an important place in their life.' Tani comments:

> The zombies appear significantly and sinisterly as consumers who, rotting and staggering, return to their earthly paradise, the only place that they have preserved in their memory. It could be added that as long as the faltering wealth of the West and the welfare state exist, consumers will consume themselves through consumption, to be finally consumed by other eager apprentice consumers arriving from the East.[16]

I wonder if you find these new-century metaphors pertinent and if any others spring to mind.

Zygmunt Bauman It's a pity I can't access Stefano Tani's original text, as it will probably be some considerable time before its English translation becomes available. From your quotations and comments, I gather that Tani is a formidable, exquisitely incisive and thoroughly original thinker with a lot of eye-opening insights to offer and share. And, to recall George Lakoff and Mark Johnson's fundamental study *Metaphors We Live By* (1980), 'metaphor is pervasive in everyday life, not just in language but in thought and action. Our ordinary conceptual system, in terms of which we both think and act, is fundamentally metaphorical in nature.' Metaphors 'govern our everyday functioning, down to the most mundane details'. Proposing three paramount metaphors most fit, in his opinion, to grasp and articulate the experience of living in the twenty-first century, Tani aims at nothing less than rethinking and updating not merely our way of thinking of the world we inhabit, but our 'everyday functioning' in it. Or, given the metaphors' power of conduct-management, he aims at assisting/streamlining the rethinking/updating labours that are already well under way.

The remarkable feature of Tani's choice is that all three proposed metaphors are ego-related. Their aim is to catch and intelligibly represent what we are nowadays inclined to think of and to do to our selves. Tani's selection assumes therefore, as well as suggests, that the preoccupations on which our thinking and acting focus are self-referential. Indeed, self-referentiality is the common denominator of all three metaphors of Tani's choice. The unmentioned – yet implied by Tani's selection – meta-metaphor, or matrix-metaphor – a synthetic metaphor of which all other metaphors of the twenty-first century metaphorics are specifications – is therefore Narcissus.

And little (if any) wonder. The meta-metaphor of the nineteenth–twentieth centuries was Pygmalion, falling in love with Galatea – a creation of his own consummate designing/performing skills. Overwhelmed with awe, wonderment and admiration, Pygmalion genuflected at the sight of the perfection of his own creative powers. Galatea stood for what humans – or, at least, the great, prodigious artists among them – can do, are doing and are determined to do with the world: with matter and spirit, with Nature and Society. She stood for the human, all too human, capability of making the world pliable and obedient to human dreams and conceptions, will and know-how. It was in those centuries that humans' historic adventure with the management of the universe reached its peak, and the adventurers felt like taking a glimpse of the other, heretofore invisible, slope of the mountain pass (to deploy Reinhardt Kosseleck's exquisite metaphor) which they climbed – facing their sanguine and boisterous premonitions with sombre, frequently gruesome and disheartening realities.

La Meta-métaphore est morte, vive la Meta-métaphore . . . With Pygmalion dethroned, the throne was vacated ready to receive his successor: Narcissus. There was no change of dynasty: Narcissus and Pygmalion were both scions of the same Promethean pedigree, famous and revered for gifts of power and comfort. But, as it happens from time to time, the coronation of the new occupant of the throne signalled change – and a radical one – in the faith and cult: now, as then, *cuius regio, eius religio* (as the supreme rulers of the day proclaimed at the threshold of the modern era, the era of rising differentiation and fragmentation concurrent with a thickening, ever more intrusive as well as obtrusive and meddlesome communication). Over the altar of the new temple no longer hovers the human-made and by-humans-managed world (whether represented by the figures of Nature or of Society), but instead its producer/manager himself – though now retired from his office and reincarnated in the figure of the world's self-focused, self-concerned consumer.

Consumer . . . Another metaphor! Its (Latin) root – 'consumere' – means 'to use up, exhaust, wear out, destroy'. Among many related meanings of the (again Latin) root of its opposite, the producer – 'producere' – are such similes as 'to bring out, bring forth, bring into the world'. Reduced to its bare essential, the opposition is between adding to, and detracting from, the world we share. Or between creating and destroying.

One of the first premonitions that the consumer was about to replace the producer in the role of the central character of society (as earlier anthropologists would have said, its 'basic personality') came already in 1955 from Victor Lebow:

> Our enormously productive economy demands that we make consumption our way of life, that we convert the buying and use of goods into rituals, that we seek our spiritual satisfactions, our ego satisfactions, in consumption. The measure of social status, of social acceptance, of prestige, is now to be found in our consumptive patterns. The very meaning and significance of our lives today are expressed in consumptive terms. The greater the pressures upon the individual to conform to safe and accepted social standards, the more does he tend to express his aspirations and his individuality in terms of what he wears, drives, eats – his home, his car, his pattern of food serving, his hobbies.[17]

Now, sixty years later, the new state of affairs has been vividly portrayed in Jacques Peretti's BBC mini-series on *The Men Who Made Us Spend*. In her review of the series, Filipa Jodelka[18] observes that 'as the program shows, our entire economy depends on this machine of perpetual spending, and civilization sort of comes to a dead end when that's buggered.'

One more reason for the figure of Narcissus being fit to replace the figure of Pygmalion and to take over the role of the meta-metaphor for the core denizen of our century: if Pygmalion fell in love with a heavy and solid sculpture carved in marble, the epitome of endurance and durability, Narcissus is infatuated with his reflection in a river – that stuff continuously on the move and a-changing, the very epitome of instability, as already Heraclitus noted in his observation that one can't enter the same river twice.

Georges Perec, later the author of *La vie: mode d'emploi*[19] – thus far, in my view, the best summary of the twentieth-century experience – was perhaps the first author to intuit the impending arrival of Narcissus – in *Les choses*.[20] Of Jérôme and Sylvie, the heroes of that novel, respectively twenty-four and twenty-two years old (young?), he wrote: 'they possessed, alas, but a single passion, the passion for a higher standard of living, and it exhausted them.'[21] As Christopher Lasch, in his *Culture of Narcissism* – the fundamental study to which I'll return later – succinctly summed up the experience of living in such a world, 'in our society, daily experience teaches the individual to want and need a never-ending supply of new toys and drugs'. Already, at the threshold of the twentieth century, Thornstein Veblen[22] spotted the prodromal symptoms of things to come, things bound to recycle Jérôme and Sylvie's life trajectories into an endless string of efforts to catch that one rung above: 'the members of each stratum', he noted, 'accept as their ideal of decency the scheme of life in vogue in the next higher stratum, and bend their energies to live up to that ideal. On pain of forfeiting their good name and their self-respect in case of failure, they must conform to the accepted code, at least in appearance.'[23] There's the rub – 'at least in appearance'. Sixty–seventy years after Veblen put this observation on paper, appearance conquered reality and conquered/colonized its realm. It rose to the status of Baudrillard's 'simulacrum', famous for effacing the difference between reality and pretence and relegating that difference to the category of Derrida's 'indécidables' – just as psychosomatic ailments wipe out the difference between disease and its make-believe. Narcissus lives in realities made, like the reflection of his face, of appearances. Narcissus earns the role of meta-metaphor in times in which appearance is the thing that really matters. In such times, it is appearances that turn into Durkheim's veritable 'social facts' (tough and immutable, as Durkheim described them – overwhelming, indomitable, non-negotiable, resistant to attempts to argue, or even wish, them away). They stay forever a step ahead of (or a rung above) me – and life for me, as for everyone (or almost everyone) else, becomes therefore a continuous – as desperate as it is doomed – effort to raise myself to their level: to the 'scheme of life in vogue'. The buck stops on my desk – as Harry Truman, facing a different but similarly structured problem, was memorably forced to assert.

Tani's metaphors of screens, Alzheimer's and Zombie, much like the feature of self-referentiality they share, can be seen as permutations rooted in (allowed by, made probable by) Narcissus' meta-metaphoric matrix. The screen referring to 'looking at oneself', Alzheimer's to 'emptying oneself', and Zombie to 'transforming oneself' stand for the defining traits/facets of Narcissus. For such activities as the existential condition of living in a society of consumers have rendered their trademark.

All our perceptions of the world 'out there' – on the outside of our body and beyond our self-image – tend to follow the pattern of 'selfies': that trick most recently technologically enabled, enthusiastically embraced and currently replacing all other, fast-ageing modes of photographic recording, with the speed of a forest fire or the Black Death. As Nicolas Rousseau recently pointed out:

> No one wishing to make a self-portrait bothers today with remote shutter release or retarders. We, the present-day narcissi, simply put our camera or 'phone in front of our face before we press the button. The camera no longer opens on the world; it brackets on us. The vanishing point is not on the horizon, at the extension of the camera-holding arm, but on our bodies.[24]

But why have we, 'the present-day narcissi', embraced the offer from the 'selfies' cameras and phones to 'bracket on us' our continuous documentary of life, with such ardour and so impetuously? I am inclined to acknowledge Christopher Lasch's explanation of this bizarre cultural turn as by far the best so far suggested. Narcissism, says Lasch, is 'the world view of the resigned'.[25]

> A society that fears it has no future is not likely to give much attention to the needs of the next generation, and the ever-present sense of historical discontinuity – the blight of our society [. . .] The perception of the world as a dangerous and forbidding place, though it originates in a realistic awareness of the insecurity of contemporary social life, receives reinforcement from the narcissistic projection of aggressive impulses outward [. . .] The cult of personal relations, which becomes increasingly intense as the hope of political solutions recedes, conceals a thoroughgoing disenchantment with personal relations, just as the cult of sensuality implies a repudiation of sensuality in all but its most primitive forms.[26]

'Experiences of inner emptiness, loneliness, and inau-
thenticity [. . .] arise from the warlike conditions (of
society), from the danger and uncertainty that surround
us, and from a loss of confidence in the future'. We are
increasingly dependent on the 'vicarious warmth provided by others combined with a fear of dependence'.
'The American cult of friendliness', Lasch concludes,
'conceals but does not eradicate a murderous competition for goods and position' – indeed for social survival
– in a world so blatantly and humiliatingly indifferent
and infuriatingly disobedient to our needs and wishes.[27]
The 'Culture of Narcissism' in the title of Lasch's
oeuvre reflects the surrender of hopes of making the
world more attentive. It sprouts and grows from the
experience of abandonment, exclusion and prospectless
loneliness; of being left to one's own, sorely inadequate,
resources; of being exiled, with no right of return except
in fantasy, from (as Freud put it in his 1914 essay *On
Narcissism*) the original paradise of 'oceanic content-
ment of the womb', which we strive for the rest of our
life to recapture – in vain, frustratingly.

We might have been doing it from the start of human
history – but never before were the dense nets of communal or familial bonds – those ingenuous, artful yet
'naturally given' substitutes for that nirvana-style bliss of
security – as unreliable, frail and torn apart by cut-throat
competition, mutual suspiciousness and enmity as they
are now. At no time was 'the tension between the desire
for union and the fact of separation'[28] so overwhelming,
hurtful and depressing; in a society where success means
not simply getting ahead but getting ahead *of others*,
there is little and ever-shrinking room left for 'personal
intimacy and social commitment', as Michael Maccoby

reports in his study of 250 managers.[29] Narcissi of our time try hard, even if only with moderate success, to get rid of that disabling tension by vacillating between two opposite stratagems. One is reunion with 'a mother' – though reincarnated in a long line of effigies veering from fundamentalist, religious or secular sects all the way to a Facebook network of 'friends'; the other, 'a state of complete self-sufficiency', 'denying any need for others at all':[30] to grin and bear it while making the best of a bad job. Both expedients are as tempting as they are ineffective, particularly as a long-term solution rather than a momentary respite. Caustically, but all-too-correctly, Jean M. Twenge and W. Keith Campbell[31] suggest that 'Narcissism is the fast food of the soul. It tastes great in the short term, has negative, even dire, consequences in the long run, and yet continues to have widespread appeal.'

Narcissus rises deservedly to the rank of the meta-metaphor in a society marked – to resort to Lasch's characterization – by the 'feeling of homelessness and displacement that afflicts so many men and women today, in their heightened vulnerability to pain and deprivation, and the contradiction between the promise that they can "have it all" and the reality of their limitations'.[32] What we are after in this sort of society is a gratifying life in a setting that is – and can't but be – independent of our wishes and yet 'responsive to our needs'. Lasch suggests that it is love and work that 'enable each of us to explore a small corner of the world and to come to accept it on its own terms. But our society tends either to devalue small comforts or else to expect too much of them [. . .] We demand too much of life, too little of ourselves.'[33]

English folk wisdom advises: 'If you can't beat them, join them.' Shouldn't Narcissus, the archetype of the consumer, in order to fulfil his ambitions and expectations, recall and relearn the by-and-large forgotten and forfeited arts of Pygmalion, the archetype of the craftsman? He can do it, on condition that the culture that promoted him to the rank of its meta-metaphor manages to shift its focus from taking to giving, from destruction to creation, from shops to love and work.

This is a Gargantuan challenge; a Herculean task. All the same, both need to be faced point-blank – and urgently. Facing them is the meta-task on which the fulfilment of all other life-tasks depends.

9
Risking Twitterature

Riccardo Mazzeo I have always admired Susan
Sontag, but after you quoted her work I felt the need
to take her books down from the shelf and re-read
them; meanwhile, reading the celebratory comments by
Sontag on the work by the Croatian writer Dubravka
Ugrečić, I bought and read Ugrečić's latest book *Karaoke
Culture*.[1] The writer chooses the Japanese word 'karaoke' (which means 'empty orchestra') – understood less
as the democratic idea 'we can all do it if we want to'
than as the democratic practice according to which 'we
all want it since we can have it' – to describe our current world, characterized by what you have defined as
a 'meta-metaphor' of contemporary existence. Here
we see Narcissus expressed not only through the inter-
polation of one's own voice over a musical base (the
Japanese 'empty orchestra'), but also as the possibility
of incarnating Tani's metaphor of reflection, emptying
and transmutation.

Today, people are more focused on escaping from
than discovering their true ego. Meantime, the ego

has become a boring concept and belongs to another culture. The possibility of transforming oneself, being subject to metamorphosis and transporting oneself into some other being or object is far more entertaining than digging down inside one's ego. The Culture of Narcissism has been transmuted into karaoke culture, or perhaps it has simply been its consequence.[2]

There is no need to recall that the Internet is responsible for the triumph of karaoke culture; it is described by Ugrečić as:

> the largest powder keg ever poured onto the eternal flame of our fantasies and imagination [. . .] like a Mao Tse-tung nightmare of a field where a hundred flowers truly do bloom [. . .] now there is a mega-karaoke where a million people grab a million microphones to sing *their personal* version of somebody else's song. Whose song? That is not important: *amnesia* seems to be a by-product of the information revolution. The important thing is *to sing*.[3]

The problems with this joyous revolution, this exalting democratization of information, education and aesthetics, are the increasingly more conspicuous erosion of any competence or expertise, the even more disturbing loss of authoritativeness, the pulverizing of any true culture, which is then recycled into a pseudo-culture. It is no accident that Professor Alan Kirby, who teaches literature in Oxford, coined the term 'pseudo-modernism' to describe a phenomenon that tends towards the unstoppable landslide of a disastrous lowering of the bar, with people – often very young – who can air their views for or against any subject under the sun, and a public that is increasingly less inclined to read books and newspapers when it is easier to put their faith in unreliable

Wikipedia and blogs. Funny and tragic at the same time is the *New Yorker* cartoon showing a dog in front of a computer commenting to another dog: 'On the internet, nobody knows you're a dog.'

There is a book by Jonathan Franzen, published between his two narrative masterpieces *The Corrections* and *Freedom*, which, although vaguely autobiographical, now and then drifts off into non-fictional reflections ... those observations that in a novel emerge mimetically from the characters perceived below the surface, through the zones of light and shade and ambivalence that exist in each of us. The title of this work is *Discomfort Zone*, and the main subject is that discomfort that is not only intrinsic to every re-birth that comes with adolescence, but that is also the source from which spring forth those mistakes and failures that are essential for creating the fatigue and frustration in life, and which, if all goes well, make it completely human. A long series of painful deliveries follow the first birth that brought us into the world, initiating challenges that have disappeared from our world, which is increasingly less courageous – deliveries that, although painful, lead to transformation, metamorphosis and development. Bypassing this discomfort means straying from the consubstantial path towards our existing in the world alongside others, their diversity, their *heteros* (ἕτερος, ἕτερο) – in short, it means non-participation in real life.

Avatars satisfy our fantasy desires to become another person in another place. Adults use them to return to childhood, which represents the quintessential *comfort zone*. The virtual world is another *comfort zone*. The adults who play *Second Life* games experience situations without risk or consequences – they fly but never fall, [. . .] they have unprotected sex [. . .]. The players have full control of their world: like gods, they are able to connect and disconnect themselves as they wish. With simulation games, juvenile *Second Life* players learn much about adult life. One little girl created herself a prostitute avatar. She said it was not such a bad thing; after all, she was not prostituting *herself*, but her avatar.[4]

The magazine *Internazionale* recently published comments by author Corinne Atlas: 'Novels are disappearing from the best seller lists in Japan.'[5] In first place is a manga, followed by several adaptations, and, as in Brazil and the United States, a large number of well-being and self-help manuals. Basically, we move from some predigested and made-easy solution to advice from 'experts' in order to learn what we need to have a better life. In fact, in her book, Ugrečić alluded to the exponential diffusion of cell-phone novels in Japan (in Japanese, *keitai shosetsu*). Here we cross over into adaptations of adaptations, or even into stories that have been barely sketched out and that are totally alien to anything that could possibly be defined as 'literature':

> Cell-phone novels are non-filtered, amateur products; the language is simplified, the plot is primitive, and the form, traditional. Generally, the heroine is a young woman from a provincial background who has to face difficult situations (she is raped, or becomes pregnant, or is abandoned by her boyfriend, etc.). Most of the authors are young women who have dropped out of school and have low educational levels.[6]

After all, if literary classics are repeatedly plundered, dismembered and made 'compatible' with the lack of culture and wavering tastes of readers led astray by those who transform *Little Women* into *Little Vampire Women*, and *Alice in Wonderland* into *Alice in Zombieland*, soon the only works worth publishing will be *twitterature*, which already has millions of social-network readers.

One footnote by Ugrečić on the subject of *Second Life* brought to mind the book by Edgar Morin, *L'Homme et la Mort*. She says:

> Since its birth, mankind has used religion to live parallel lives with passion and devotion. Only 2.2 billion Christians in the world today believe in the SL [*Second Life*] story. The fact that the SL computer game differs slightly from the religious concept is unimportant. The fact is that the human brain is always ready to transport itself into another world. So even the theory that Google is the Almighty becomes a little more plausible.[7]

In his book in 1951, Morin offered a powerful and astute anthropological insight into human attitudes towards death, and two principal concepts put forward in support of his argument: dualism and death–rebirth. These two forms of escape – while not from death itself, but the *idea* of death – have always existed, transfigured in very disparate ways, interwoven in rock-hard philosophical systems, even ready to spring forth now and then from the atheism of Feuerbach.

In Communism, this was incarnated in the belief in earthly salvation, and people were ready to sacrifice themselves for a future better and fairer world; in the most fertile periods of Catholicism, the poor were easily manipulated and maintained in a passive status quo thanks to the precept 'Render unto Caesar the things that are Caesar's', consoling them with the hope of an afterlife where 'the last shall be first'. It was relatively easy to impose obedience on the masses when they were proposed a project, an expectation, a faith – whether this was placed in God, dictatorship by the proletariat, science or technology. It was also simple to channel the rage beating in human hearts and direct it towards the 'enemy' in the Fascist myth of *ius soli* and race, as do the radical Islamists today or many modern Russians who are still firm believers in the vainglory of Great Mother Russia (a Russian friend of mine whom you have met, and who is far from being a fanatic in many other respects, often nostalgically dreams of the Great Russian Army, the music and speeches of the Empire, and the military parades). In our Western world emptied of any form of future project planning or any faith, submerged by Pygmalion's plunge into the pool of Narcissus, divested of any values or sensibility, what remains if not the karaoke pseudo-culture created by *wannabes*, *Doppelgängers*, *look-alikes* and *avatars*?

Zygmunt Bauman Many years ago, I suggested that, instead of talking about identity, we should rather, when wishing to grasp the mode of being-in-the-world nowadays prevailing, speak of identification: of a never-ending effort, uninterrupted except for a brief moment of rest at the nearest roadside inn; an effort never finished, forever in the course of becoming. Perhaps we should add to our linguistic toolbox, as a replacement for the 'avatar', a clumsy and graceless word, 'avatarizing', standing for an updated version of the concept of 'reincarnation': the concept enthusiastically rediscovered and, not without reason, adapted and heartily embraced by the cults of Oriental wisdom so popular among the denizens of the liquid-modern world. An updated version, I repeat – as reincarnation was something that happened to us without our knowledge, let alone control, and was oblivious to our longings and preferences, whereas 'avatarization' refers to what we want to do, and are doing, the way we desire. To 'avatarize' means what you quote from *Karaoke Culture*: 'we all want it since we can have it'. Or, rather, 'since it is available for having' – more precisely, 'since it is available for purchase', because what the formula you quoted omits to mention, is the gap between 'being available for having through purchasing' and 'I can have it': a distance passable solely in the vehicles of bank accounts and credit cards. That distance is not just a nasty, often exasperating and sometimes incapacitating impairment, but also the principal source of the élan vital to the consumerist economy.

Choosing, as I insist *ad nauseam*, is the sole ingredient of the liquid-modern life itinerary that is not a matter of choice. Once a privilege, choice has by now turned into a must – a duty you can neither refuse nor shirk and evade. Besides, 'reincarnation' is an event that occurs but once in a lifetime – whereas 'avatarization' is in principle capable of happening daily, hourly; such a happening is, moreover, eminently suitable to multitasking. In addition, with a reincarnation, one is encumbered for life – whereas avatarization one can practise as long as one lives. Willy-nilly, Max Weber comes to mind: namely, his distinction between a steel casing and a light cloak that can be dropped from your shoulders at a moment's notice and replaced by another – though, as in Weber's story of Puritan ethics in which that metaphor was employed, light cloaks have an awesome potency (and inclination!) of hardening into steel casings.

'We are nothing, let us be all', the converts to Communism used to sing in their anthem, 'The Internationale', while calling the oppressed and the miserable to abandon hope of salvation from the top, focusing instead 'on saving ourselves'. Following Edgar Morin, you point out that Communism tempted/cajoled people to be ready to 'sacrifice themselves for a future better and fairer world' with the vision of earthly salvation. Like the reincarnation promised by Oriental teachings, so the prospect of salvation displayed to its followers by Marxism, as much as by Christian faith, was to be a one-off, irrevocable and irreversible transmutation, a passage akin to crossing the River Styx, famous for barring return. A one-way street, so to speak. This is what the advent of avatarization, carried on the tides of modernity's liquidization, changed to the core. What it brought instead was a phasing-out of the bane of finality and consequentiality of choices, decisions, engagements and undertakings; putting paid to 'fateful choices' and keeping one's trajectory at a safe distance from 'points of no return'; drastic reduction – and, in a growing number of cases, elimination – of risks attached to choices and decisions; the increasing possibility of returning to the starting point after an unsuccessful run, and of starting anew while effacing the records of false starts in the past; cancelling that 'staying power of the moment' (of which Nietzsche's Zarathustra complained in the name of the Superman whose imminent arrival he announced), that cause of much horror, wrath and teeth-gnashing in the fans of transmuting adventures – and, all in all, disarming the past of its hold on the present. Or at least the chance of hoping that disarmament can be achieved, and pretending that it has been: by all means, a priceless boon to the strong- and weak-hearted alike. Yet the gain it offers does not consist in showing, let alone guaranteeing, the right way; instead, it lies in stripping the choice of a way – whatever way has been, or is wished to be, chosen – from the curse of irrevocability. Just try, try and try again. More than in trying correctly, the art of life consists in never abandoning the trying.

That tremendous departure was and continues to be acclaimed as a gigantic leap forward in the ages-long struggle for autonomy – and the right to, as well as capability of, self-assertion. You quote from Dubravka Ugrečić': 'The adults who play *Second Life* games [games of fantasy: toying with the designing of imaginary selves and roles in search for the one promising the maximum of gratification – followed by adopting them for public presentation of the player's self] experience situations without risk or consequences [. . .] The players have full control of their world: like gods, they are able to connect and disconnect themselves as they wish'. Behind that enchantment with 'full control' over wide open vistas, there is a thoroughly comforting feeling of 'no risk involved'. Why no risk? Not because one can be sure of a felicitous outcome – but because there will always be another chance. One is able to freely wind up a not fully gratifying episode to vacate the site for another.

There is big money behind that claim pouring from every loudspeaker and advertising board. And no wonder: incessant avatarization and re-avatarization, each successive avatar stopping short of perfection and calling for the next exercise in transmutation, is the surest, most effective remedy against the menace of a 'satisfied consumer' – satisfied through not being exposed to 'new and improved' temptations, or because novel attractions fail to trigger in him or her new desires or wants masquerading as 'needs' or 'musts'. One can perhaps go as far as concluding that the infinity of personality choices on offer and insatiability of the lust for 'new starts' and the dream of 'being born again' combine currently into the main fly-wheel of consumerist economy.

'Avatars satisfy our fantasy desires to become another person in another place', suggests Dubravka Ugrečić.[8] 'Avatars can take whatever shape or form a user chooses.'[9] As the practitioners of karaoke, that wondrous technological appliance that puts the capacity to use an instant avatar within everybody's – or nearly everybody's – reach, maintain: 'with their avatars they feel a greater freedom (the word they use most frequently) than they do in the real world'.[10] I would add to Ugrečić's observation: karaoke cuts down considerably the costs of avatarization – the karaoke version of the avatar is many times cheaper and requires much less learning, skills, time and effort in laborious preparations than did its pre-karaoke versions. Moreover, it renders avatarization safer: karaoke virtually (in both meanings of that last word) abolishes the risks of experimentation, or even the need to stretch the imagination beyond most of its willing/aspiring practitioners' talents and capacity. Karaoke is like IKEA furniture: it comes with the pieces and design sketches you can rely on – what is left to you is to follow the sketch and put the pieces

together according to the attached drawing. Full satis-
faction is guaranteed: the joys of craftsmanship without
the hazards of unmapped territory and the perils of the
unknown. One is offered the delights of being someone
else without the jeopardy of cutting a comic figure – or
somewhere else without the danger of losing your way.
What is on offer is nothing less than the best of both
worlds – freedom and security in one package deal: the
eternal dream of reconciling the two values, both hotly
desired yet stubbornly at loggerheads, finally fulfilled.
This, I suggest, is karaoke's main attraction – and the
cause of the astounding success of the consumerist
economy in its efforts to recut its offers after karaoke's
pattern – as well as a reason to judge Ugrečić's decision to define our current lifestyle as 'karaoke culture'
phenomenally felicitous.

The Internet, Ugrečić points out, can be understood as
'a mega-karaoke where a million people grab a million
microphones to sing *their personal* version of somebody
else's song. Whose song? That is not important [. . .]
The important thing is *to sing*.'[11] This is important to
both those who set the tunes and those millions who
wouldn't sing if tunes were not set. 'The Internet, like
a giant vacuum cleaner, sucks up absolutely everything,
including the canons.'[12] Well, not exactly everything.
The dream, desire and will to grab mics were born
long, long before the Internet – or even the mics – had
been invented. The astonishing – well-nigh instant –
success of the Internet in lifting karaoke to the rank
of a fitting metaphor of culture is due to the fact that
this dream, desire and will were already there, hiber-
nating or dozing for the lack of effective tools and the
courage to venture out in the absence of safe vehicles

– yet waiting ever more impatiently to be released and capitalized on.

Take Siegfried Kracauer, 'Die Reise und der Tanz' ('Travel and Dance') published originally almost a century ago in *Frankfurter Zeitung* on 15 March 1925: 'The goal of modern travel is not its destination but rather a new place as such [. . .] Though at present the exotic may still cling to the pyramids and the Golden Horn, someday it will designate any spot in the world whatsoever, to the extent that the spot appears unusual from the perspective of any other point in the world'; 'travel is of the sort that above all and most of the time has no particular destination; its meaning is exhausted in the mere fact of changing location'.[13] Let me remind you of Ugrečić's findings: what is important is that we sing, it does not matter what songs. In both cases, today as 100 years ago, we experience being someone else, somewhere else. Dreams did not progress, only the technology of fantasizing their fulfilment did. The present-day mass-produced and designed-for-mass-consumption digital technology provides moulds into which we pour our formless fantasies to acquire shape, riverbeds for the ensuing actions to flow, grooves fixing the estuary. In karaoke culture, the urge to self-expression supplies the energy, while profit-seeking markets supply the matter. Electronic technology supplies both the form and the contents of both thought and action, while assuring that – far from nearing exhaustion due to their intense consumption – the volumes of energy and matter continue to grow, outpacing the rise in demand.

And thank God, history or the marketers' acumen and gumption for all that – given the state of *horror vacui* into which Kracauer predicted our contemporaries would be cast, having first traced the way in which the modern self 'developed in its struggle to attain autonomy', rounded up subsequently 'into a highly expressive, unique personality of Romanticism' – until, in the age of materialism and capitalism, 'both become ever more atomized and increasingly degenerate into an arbitrary chance construct'; 'These people are struck by the curse of isolation and individuation [. . .] Since these people lack ties and firm ground, their spirit/intellect drifts along without direction, at home everywhere and nowhere.'[14] Are we not to be thankful to the providers of those moulds, riverbeds and grooves that point out to us – perplexed as we are – the right direction? And they do that without preventing us from being at home everywhere and nowhere, thereby insuring (or at least promising to insure) us against that nasty trauma that eviction from home – that all-too-real prospect in the world of materialism, capitalism and liquid modernity – would have surely caused.

10
Dry and Damp

Riccardo Mazzeo   In the previous chapter, we discussed the progressive cancellation of literature that goes hand in hand with the current trend towards abolishing any form of effort and the hyper-simplification favoured by new technologies, plus the unrestrained suppression of any form of in-depth exploration – surfing instead of fathoming. In short, this confirms Racine's expression 'le plus profond c'est la peau' – the *Writing Degree Zero* of language and perception reduced to their most rudimental and immediate elements. This tacky production must be of interest to the sociologist and must cause some concern, although it is obvious it will not be of any help.

However, literature is steadfast and die-hard, and, now and then, a novel appears that offers sensitive evidence of concepts that, incarnated by the characters, confirm reality in a way that is much more powerful than any dissertation. I refer to Michel Houellebecq's dystopia *The Possibility of an Island*, the vibrant re-proposal of Albert Camus' *The Plague* – *Blindness* by

Saramago – and the supine complying with injunctions from above in the perpetration of all the horror described by Jonathan Littell in *The Kindly Ones*. I recently read a novel by an Italian author, Alberto Garlini, *The Law of Hate*.[1] It is almost as long as Littell's saga and, I feel, animated by the attempt to explain mythically the roots of Fascism.

Garlini later told me that, in reality, his initial project was to write a book centred around Bruce Chatwin and his passion for nomadism. However, at a certain point, as a contrast he decided to introduce a Fascist, a character that was Chatwin's complete opposite. However, he did not know any Fascists, and was not very familiar with Fascist movements. So he began researching, studying documents, interviews and non-fiction. This frenzied research coagulated in Stefano, the main character, a twenty-year-old, full of resentment and a remote but long-lasting sense of guilt as a result of a series of what Charles Wright Mills calls *troubles*: the difficulties that 'occur within the character of the individual and within the range of his immediate relations with others',[2] and that, in order to be understood and managed appropriately, should be connected with *issues*, those problems common to many other human beings. However, like most normal people, Stefano remains blocked by his own terribly thorny personal problems: a bankrupt and drunken father, insulted and deceived by everyone and especially those who pretended to be his friends, and a good, hard-working mother who was forced to prostitute herself occasionally to provide for the family. When he was small, Stefano's father would take him fishing, and on one occasion when he was in a totally drunken state:

he started to eat the worms. He took handfuls and dropped them down his throat. It was horrible to see him eat that slimy stuff.

'I am like your mother', he said to Stefano while he was chewing. 'Only she eats the worms that come out of men's peckers. You were born from one of those worms. And it wasn't even an Italian worm. He used to say *alright* and sang like Frank Sinatra'. He grabbed the last handful of worms, crushed them in his mouth and yelled: 'Bastard!' Then he vomited his heart up in the lake. The trout came up to the surface to gobble the pink slush that was spreading on the water.[3]

Stefano grows up among Fascists. His father is a Fascist. Rocco, the person who replaces his father after his true father's death (and who continues to be his mother's occasional lover) is a Fascist. Mixing reality and fantasy in events that occurred between 1968 and 1971, Garlini describes the bombing in Piazza Fontana (which took place in Milan in December 1969, killing seventeen people and injuring eighty-eight) from the perspective of Stefano who, manipulated by high-level Fascists in league with deviated members of public institutions, places the bomb himself. He is convinced that the bomb will explode without harming bystanders and instead finds himself betrayed and used like his parents. Stefano is violent and a murderer but the author attributes him with characteristics that are so human and, in some ways, heroic that they render him identifiable; readers can identify with him, and see him not as an enemy on the opposite side of the barricades, but as able to inspire strong feelings of empathy. In the novel (in a fictitious meeting imagined by the author), Julius Evola defines

Stefano as a 'Blue wolf' and throws him out of his house. Stefano asks his fiancée, Antonella, what the expression means, and she explains that 'in Indo-European communities, the exiles, the expelled, the people who are banned, basically all those who do not conform to the dominant ethos', were defined in this way: 'They represented a rarity compared to the normal grey wolves. Terrible, but also captivating. As an example, think of certain comic strip criminals. Think of Diabolik. A thief and a murderer. Despicable, but charismatic.'[4]

In reality, it is easy to become attached to Stefano as a character, especially in comparison to the Fascists who surround him and who manoeuvre the boys whom they consider as cannon fodder. He is pure and innocent, and harbours a spasmodic (and comprehensible) need to rise up towards cleaner air than in the rubbish dump in which he has lived. His needs are absorbed by the mirage of a nobler and more orderly world, a world where worms do not have citizen status, where the shame of his family is replaced by pride, even at the risk of his life. When he accidentally kills a young contemporary, Mauro, his world falls apart:

> He had thought he was capable of killing. He imagined it was relatively simple, in fact – the duty of a political soldier. He had wanted it with every single spark of energy. He knew it was only a question of time and that it would happen. But nothing happened as he had expected. There was no battle. The victim was not a warrior. The knife blade had penetrated deeply without any reason, without motivation. Mauro's predisposition as a victim. The death of an innocent victim is an insult to honour. A cavalier's duty is to protect the innocent, not to kill them.[5]

Unfortunately, for him there is no redemption. Thanks to the twin sister of his involuntary victim, with whom he falls in love in a desperate and improper attempt at compensation; thanks to the verses of an Argentinian poetess, friend of the twins, whose poetry Stefano learns by heart and is, in certain moments, inspired and sustained by; but, most of all, thanks to the meeting with Chatwin who electrifies him by speaking of 'Cain the farmer, just like Hitler, who hated the Jews because they were a nomadic people'[6] and also about the prehistoric feline dinofelis which, contrary to the beliefs of anthropologists, was the true perpetrator of ancient pierced skulls, and not man – Stefano undergoes a profound transformation. He manages to forgive his mother and to understand her motivations:

> She was a woman to be pitied. She had worked her fingers to the bone, had accepted every kind of compromise to feed and educate her son. In her humble mind, she imagined that this handsome strong son might even manage to be happy, but the opposite occurred: her sacrifices and the resulting sense of guilt made Stefano angry and violent until this silenced every other feeling that was not hatred towards the whole world. But how could she have known it? How could she have imagined that her sheep-like mildness would become the raw blade of the knife her son carried hidden in his pocket?[7]

But the *troubles* of the main character cannot be resolved simply through his belated acquisition of awareness: his *issues* continue to exist and attack, and, just as a single person cannot resolve the problems of the world through his own efforts without resorting to politics and acting *together* with others, in the same way, Stefano is not able to overturn the intrigues that loom over him and the cruel and strategically honed, merciless drive used to manipulate him. After his rebellion, he is hunted down until he draws his last breath.

Believe that this and other similar books that twitterature will not be able to annihilate with ease constitute nutritious food for thought for both sociologists and the masses alike.

Zygmunt Bauman A Fascist father eating worms in front of his Fascist son, as a demonstration – of what? Obviously, of what needs to / will be done with/to disgusting and revolting creatures, vile and loathsome because they are slimy. Jean-Paul Sartre picked *le visqueux* – the 'slimy' – as a metaphor of the simultaneously slippery and sticky nature of the human condition: an aporetic condition, hopelessly out of control; a condition disallowing both adherence and separation, resisting embrace while simultaneously refusing to let go – and for that reason repellent and nauseating. Father packs worms in his mouth not to digest them, but to vomit; showing thereby that they can't be held in, that their destination predestined at the moment of entry is to be disgorged. In *Les tristes tropiques* (1955), Claude Lévi-Strauss suggested that there are but two ways in which cultures tend to tackle the issue of the 'others', 'different' and 'foreign': the anthropophagic strategy – 'eating up' the differences or their carriers and thus 'assimilating' the foreign elements, peeling and divesting them of their 'esoterism'; and the 'anthropoemic' strategy – 'vomiting' them: expelling, eliminating, destroying. Leaving nothing to doubt, the father reminds his son that he himself, like other humans, originated from sperm, a slimy substance. The sperm disgorged to conceive him not being even Italian, it must have been, so to speak, doubly slimy – an allusion, I presume, to the ideas of 'Mischling' and 'Rassenschande', imported from the Nazi vocabulary: such phenomena as threaten to dilute, and eventually wash out, identities of nations and/or races, and so create a foggy and oozy area of ambivalence at a space where unequivocal and impassable borders need to / must be drawn – a menace making the oddity and the threat of sliminess yet more sinister and daunting. The separation and keeping apart of the solid from the slimy is a challenge and a task with which Stefano is burdened; Stefano's life will be devoted to fulfilling that task, portending in his case a particularly tiresome and weary uphill struggle.

In *Le sec et l'humide* ('Dry and Damp'), a study published by Gallimard two years after *Les bienveillantes* (translated into English under the title of 'The Kindly Ones', instead of the more adequate 'Well-wishers'), Jonathan Littell tried to unpack the worldview and mentality of Léon Degrelle, the commander of the Belgian 'SS Wallonie' division and one of the archetypal figures in the gallery of Nazi types. Littell pursued his investigation by focusing on the vocabulary – and through it on the conceptual framework – deployed by Degrelle in his memoirs, published in 1949 under the title *La campagne de Russie*. In pursuing his subject, Littell draws profusely on Klaus Theweleit's *Männerphantasien* study of 1977.[8] Like Theweleit, Littell questions the applicability to the Fascist case of Freud's id-ego-superego model of personality, with its Oedipus complex as the principal category deployed in the reconstitution of personality dynamics; he prefers to ground that case on Melanie Klein's and Margaret Mahler's childhood psychoanalysis. The Fascist – so Littell suggests (26–9) following Theweleit's propositions – 'never achieves separation from his mother', and 'remains forever yet-unborn'.[9] The Fascist is not a psychopath; he effects, 'alas, frequently effectively', a 'substitute separation' – constructing 'with the help of discipline, drill, physical exercise, an exteriorised self taking the form of a "carapace"'. The carapace, however, is never hermetic, the 'carapace self' tends to be fragile, and the Fascist lives perpetually under the threat of a 'dissolution of personal boundaries'. To survive, he needs to exteriorize the dangers in order to kill in effigy the internal sources of disruption: elements of the never-fully-rid-of feminine (opposite to 'the male') and the 'liquid' (the opposite of the stable and 'solid'). We may say that such a separating operation represents the universe as a battlefield between two Manichaean elements separated by a long series of oppositions: all of them being permutations of the meta-oppositions between order and chaos (or solid ground and bog) – or, indeed, as the title implies, between 'dry' and 'damp'. 'To structure himself, the Fascist needs to structure the world' – to render the world neatly divided after the pattern of his metaphors. And he does, with the help of such oppositions as those between rigid and formless, tough and soft, immovable and flowing, tough and flaccid, clean and unclean, clean-shaven and hairy, bright and misty, transparent and opaque, etc.[10] Division between objects of love or friends/allies/companions inside the safe shelter of *chez soi*, and the objects of hatred and repulsion, follows. Metaphors act as Austin's perlocutions or Merton's self-fulfilling prophecies – their aim being to conjure up orderliness in randomness, transparency in fog: in the nutshell, to put things where they belong. Your mother – so the father instructs his son in Garlini's novel – eats worms; I vomit them. In that behavioural difference between male and female, what is the cause and what is the effect in this opposition-ridden world of ours?

Analysing the intricate mechanisms of the Fascist psyche is as indomitable a task as it is fascinating. Here, as in so many other areas of investigating human existence and coexistence, cooperation between the social sciences and literature was as effective as it was earnest. Novel-writers Littell and Garlini found in academic researchers Melanie Klein and Margaret Mahler or Klaus Theweleit superb companions-in-arms in the battle they all waged, whether separately or shoulder-to-shoulder. My doubts, however, concern the selection of the topic in that wider campaign – the search for pragmatically useful (that is, translatable into the language of policies) answers to the question *unde malum?* – and so, consequently, the crucial question of the ways in which evil could be fought. As you know however, I suspect that focusing on the psychological predispositions of evil-doers, as distinct from the social causes of the evil-doers' proliferation, may well result in disablement instead of enabling us to carry on that fight effectively. That focusing, willy-nilly, tends to set the evil-doers apart as mutants, while exonerating the rest of us of guilt and absolving us from the urge to do something about the world which we create while being by it created. Even Evola files Stefano into the 'Blue wolves' category . . .

The self – formless, soft, flowing, flaccid and unclean as manifested in its deeds and misdeeds – tends in that world to be 'outsourced' to make room for the rigid, tight, tough and solid, expertly moulded and cast armour, offering – just like Theweleit/Littell's 'carapace' – effective protection against the torments of the moral judgement and painful pangs of conscience. To use my preferred terms: instead of acting as the laboratory in which decisions about how and where to move are recycled into moral problems, the self is turning now, as in the case of the Fascist men, into a factory of adiaphorization. The only news is the volume and reach of its production. Not much more than a cottage industry in the days of ideology and the *Führerprinzip*, it has risen in market times to the level of mass-production industrial plants. Once manned by self-selected and/or targeted-for-commissioning 'soldatische Männer', the present-day industry of adiaphorization marks us all as employees or job applicants. It is true – and not at all insignificant – that the managers, their philosophy and their style of action in each of the two eras differ sharply; but it is also true that, in both cases, the most effective supplier of the objects of their management was and remains the existential condition of uncertainty, insecurity, perplexity and haplessness: of 'remaining forever yet-unborn'.

11

The Retrenchment Within 'Oneness'

Riccardo Mazzeo In fact, you referred to Jonathan Littell's book *Les bienveillantes* (*The Kindly Ones*) in your essay *A Natural History of Evil* (2012), to explain how evil is something far more widespread, pervasive and contagious than we would believe possible to imagine just from looking at a gallery of specific individuals like degenerates, sadists and violent psychopaths. You had already discussed this in one of your earlier works, *Modernity and The Holocaust* (1989), and the scalpel of your intelligence was even more incisive in your recent essay, in which you spoke of the progressive wildfire diffusion of callousness whereby economic factors take precedence (e.g., the money spent in perfecting the atomic bomb) over the enormous waste of human lives in Hiroshima and Nagasaki – a tragedy that was not at all necessary, given that Japan was on the point of surrender ('but we can't throw away 2 million dollars-worth of work . . .'). Such insensitivity can transform a nice, kind, talented boy from provincial America (or any other country) into a monster like the torturers at Abu

Grahib whenever the circumstances (the context, influence of others, dehumanization of the enemy) permit.

I admired Littell's very powerful narrative and reread it because I believe that, beyond the psychological analysis of the main character (or of Degrelle in Littell's later essay *Le sec et l'humide* ('Dry and Damp'), it communicates more general and important aspects for human sciences. After ten years spent in the most devastated zones of war and massacre in the world, this author, of Russian origin, born in New York, with a passion for French literature, requested French nationality for himself, his wife and two daughters. Initially refused, he was granted French citizenship with full honours after the enormous success of his book. His desire to throw himself heart and soul into his subject forced him to go to experience personally the places where evil had been at its most ferocious in order to try and understand it; he then wrote over 1,000 pages in his favourite language, and finally went to live in the country he felt so drawn to. In short, he tried to see things from within, and, in *Les bienveillantes*, he made the Herculean effort to assume the character and speak with the voice of an SS officer who was responsible for many horrors of the Holocaust: a man who had simply wanted to study literature and play the piano, but who – despite certain doubts, remorse and even strong physical malaise over the atrocities he was committing – did not hesitate to kill, and even plan the extermination of, innocent people, including women and children.

In our conversation centred on the importance of literature in understanding others, I feel that this work deserves further discussion because it almost seems that the author had absorbed your thoughts on the subject and wished to support them with sensitive evidence by incarnating them in the characters of his book.

Already in the first few pages, he makes statements that seem to paraphrase comments you made fifteen years beforehand: 'Of course, the war is over. And we have learnt the lesson, it will not happen again. But are you really sure we have learnt the lesson? Are you sure it will never happen again? Are you even truly convinced that the war is over?'[1] It is impossible not to hear the echo of your comments on the Death Factory (genocide) when you said that it not only can be reopened, it has probably never been closed.

Rereading the book seven years later, I found another important echo, exquisitely literary, but perhaps also relevant to sociology – it is the work by Robert Musil that recalls the twin sister of the main character of *Les bienveillantes*: Maximilian Aue's sister, Una. Max is a homosexual. He had actual sexual relations with his twin sister for a certain time when they were young until, after discovery of this by their parents, Max was sent away to boarding school. In *Les bienveillantes* Max describes the origin of his sexual orientation:

> I loved a woman. Only one, but more than any other thing in the world. And yet, she was the one woman who was forbidden to me. It is very easy to understand that in dreaming of being a woman, dreaming of having a woman's body, I kept searching for her, I wanted to be near her, I wanted to be like her, I wanted to be her.[2]

In the works of art, he finds only his lost sister:

> I needed only to walk past a portrait of a woman with thick black hair for my imagination to strike me like an axe; and

even when the face looked nothing like hers, under the rich gowns of the Renaissance or Regency periods, under those brightly coloured fabrics studded with gems, as thick as the glowing oils of the artist, it was her body I saw, her breasts, her belly, her beautiful hips that enveloped her bones or were slightly rounded, and that enclosed the only source of life that I was able to identify with.[3]

In Musil's great uncompleted novel, identification with the beloved assumes a different tone: everything is more analytical and refined; there is no reference to sexual identification or physical relations. Even the description of the commonality between the two twins, who, like Max and Una, were separated in childhood, living far away from each other for many years, has a different configuration: 'Ulrich observed Agathe's face once again. It did not seem to resemble his own face very much; but perhaps he was mistaken, perhaps it was similar – rather like a pastel sketch or a wooden sculpture, so that the difference in material did not reveal the similarity in the features and texture.'[4]

However, the ghost of total identification appears in Musil's work as well. For example, he recalls when they were children and Agathe was dressed up for a ball: 'She wore a velvet gown and her hair flowed over it like waves of pale velvet, and although he too was dressed up like a terrible chevalier, suddenly the sight [of Agathe] made him wish he was a girl.'[5] However, this identification returns like a flash of light when they meet again as adults after the death of their father: 'It was as if he saw himself appear on the threshold coming towards him; but more beautiful and bathed in a splendour that he had never seen in himself. For the first time he was struck by the thought that his sister was an imaginary repetition and transformation of himself.'[6]

I feel that the aspect that emerges from the books of Musil and Littell is the search for the *equal same*, the unsuccessful castration performed by the law of language which, as you stated together with Gustavo Dessal in *El retorno del péndulo* ('The Return of the Pendulum'),[7] is essential in order to open up to *heteros*, or that other person, because (s)he is different from ourselves. The stagnation of the identical, of the ossified ideal model, can refer to single anorexic cases hiding behind the denial of everything external, structuring themselves as autonomous in their assertion against the rest of the world, but it can also involve an entire people who come together in a single entity (a race for the Nazis, and a class for Russian Communism) to make a stand within its perfection. On this subject, Littell creates a dialogue between Maximilian Aue and a Russian prisoner who is as intelligent and aware as he is himself, in order to underline the similarities between their systems. The prisoner says:

> Where Communism aims at a classless society, you preach *Volksgemeinschaft*, which, in the end, is exactly the same thing, limited within your borders. Where Marx saw the proletariat as the bearer of truth, you have decided that the so-called German race is a proletarian race, the incarnation of Good and morality; consequently, you have replaced the German proletarian war against capitalistic states.[8]

Both systems are revealed as strenuously deterministic – since human beings are *other-directed*, the 'objective enemies' must be eliminated: categories of people who must be eradicated, not because of their actions or beliefs, but because of the very fact of being what they are.

> In this, we differ only on the definition of these categories: for you these are the Jews, the Roma, the Poles, and even, if I understand correctly, the mentally ill; for us it is the Kulaki, the Bourgeoisie, the deviationists from the Party. In the end it is the same thing; both reject the capitalistic *homo oeconomicus*, self-centred, egotistical, individualistic, victim of his illusions of freedom, in favour of a *homo faber*.[9]

The radical nature of this approach is the result of suffering and resentment. We see it evolving today in situations where material and moral conditions are collapsing, giving rise to a revival of Fascism even in Greece, where, alongside the success of Tsipras, there is an extreme right-wing movement flexing its muscles together with its consensus. Retrenchment within 'oneness', the fortified defence of one's own state against all others, is visible even among those who, until yesterday, were the victims of persecution: the Jews of the state of Israel. At a certain point, Mandelbrod, an influential friend of Maximilian's father, says:

> What is more *völkisch* than Zionism? Just as we did, they too realised that *Volk* and *Blut* cannot exist without *Boden*, and so the Jews must be sent back to the land of *Eretz Yisrael* pure of any other race. [...] The Jews are the original true National Socialists and date back almost three and a half thousand years, ever since Moses gave them the Law to separate them from other peoples forever. All our fundamental ideas come from the Jews, and we must have the lucidity to admit this: The Land both as promised and

as completion, the notion of the chosen people among all others, the concept of purity of blood. [. . .] And it is for this reason that, among our enemies, the Jews are the worst and most dangerous of all; they are the only ones truly worth hating. They are our only true competition. Our only real rivals.[10]

Alberto Garlini once told me that the population of Israel reminded him of the Italians: a collection of people so different from one another, intelligent, creative, in permanent reciprocal conflict and governed by politicians who are far from being authentic representatives of most of the population. If I think of two Israeli citizens whom I had the privilege to meet with you, David Grossman and Abraham Yehoshua, so wonderfully prolific, poetic and humane in their work, I can only be delighted with such a comparison. However, the danger of the opposition between *oneness* and the rest of the world exists, and has borne (and continues to bear) poisoned fruit like the ghettoization of the Palestinians.

Oneness reminds me of a passage in your book with Gustavo Dessal: 'Sartre was wrong, while Freud was right: hell is not other people, although there are certain "others" able to create infernal suffering quite efficiently. It is only inasmuch as this hell exists within ourselves that we can permit a certain hopeful state of mind that allows us to be convinced that the hell is outside ourselves.'[11] It is only by opening up to others, by recognizing and accepting their diversity as the fruit of our common humanity that we can save ourselves from our own inferno. I think that Littell expresses this thought especially well through the words of his main character:

If the horrendous massacres of Eastern Europe prove anything, it is precisely and paradoxically the terrifying unchanging solidarity of mankind. However brutalized and however accustomed they became, not one of our men was able to kill a Jewish woman without thinking of his own wife, sister or mother. Nor could they kill a Jewish child without seeing their own children in the graves in front of them. Their reactions, their violence, their depression, their suicides, my own sadness . . . all these aspects demonstrated that the *other* exists; (s)he exists as another person, as a human being, and that no volition, no ideology, no dose of stupidity or alcohol can break this tenuous but indestructible bond. This is not an opinion, but a fact.[12]

Zygmunt Bauman   Max and Una, Ulrich and Agathe . . . those two couples beg to be cast against the more capacious backcloth of Lévi-Strauss' *Les structures élémentaires de la parenté* (1949). Claude Lévi-Strauss traces back the origins of culture – all culture – to the prohibition of incest: the point at which nature and culture met and a buckle fastening together nature and culture was formed, and a long – indeed perpetual – cultural routine of refashioning natural features into cultural distinctions and culturally mediated social divisions was launched. '[S]he was the one woman who was forbidden to me': so moans/laments Max Aue when confessing his feelings for his sister Una. Culture imposes differences upon blandly indifferent nature. As far as nature goes, all women are fit for sexual intercourse; the idea of exempting sisters from that universal rule is a cultural artefact fashioned from the natural fact of shared parentage. From then on, so Lévi-Strauss suggests, a similar stratagem has been repeatedly used in the workings of culture – for instance, to set aside *unwertes Leben* from the lives worthy of survival, an underclass from the society of classes, an un-race from the world of races. Picking up the traits that matter from the universe of traits that don't, classifying and categorizing, dividing people and differentiating their merits and rights, are paramount preoccupations and accomplishments of culture. In this way, culture enables and constrains, and/or incapacitates. Littell and Musil return to the mythical roots from which that preoccupation and that accomplishment sprouted. Following Amartya Sen and Martha Nussbaum, Richard Sennett points out some of their mature products: 'Human beings are capable of doing more than schools, workplaces, civil organizations and political regimes allow for ... People's capacities for cooperation are far greater and more complex than institutions allow them to be'[13] ... institutions, culture's artefacts, reserve the right to allow and disallow.

Joke Brouwer and Sjoerd van Tuinen aver in the preface to the book they jointly edited – though with a tad excessive sanguinity – that 'Under a thin layer of consumerism lies an ocean of generosity'[14] (by the way, that vision is strikingly reminiscent of Victor Turner's conceptual couple *societas* and *communitas*, or structure and anti-structure, introduced in his *Ritual Passage* study of 1969 – standing for perpetually co-present, intertwining and interpenetrating modes of existence). Peter Sloterdijk, referring to Marcel Mauss' classic study of the gift, insists, in one of the interviews included in Brouwer and van Tuinen's book,[15] that the giving in question is not just a spontaneous outburst of generosity; it is also experienced by the giver as an obligation

– though an obligation free from grudge and resentment, its fulfilment hardly ever experienced or thought of as an act of self-deprivation or self-sacrifice. In the case of a gift true to its nature, the common opposition between egoism and altruism is cancelled. That opposition is dissolved, we may say, in the state/condition/mentality/ambiance of companionship and solidarity. To give means *doing* good, but also *feeling* good; the outward and inward, altruistic and egoistic aspects of the do-good impulse, merge and are no longer distinguishable from each other – let alone at loggerheads.

Sloterdijk goes on to suggest the coexistence of two economies: erotic and thymotic. (Let me explain that the concept of the second kind of economy takes a leaf from Plato's idea of 'thymos': the third part of the soul alongside *logos* (mind) and *pathos* (animist appetites), *thymos* stands for self-esteem and the hunger for recognition – it is, we may say, the essentially 'socializing' factor in the human psyche, active in connecting one to the many, I to thou or it, the interior and exterior aspects of existence. It has been suggested by Plato's interpreters that man's humanity flourishes most when he transcends survivalist, materialist inclinations and engages his thymotic side, but also that 'thymos is what motivates the best and worst things men do'.[16]) 'The erotic economy', Sloterdijk suggests:

> is not just driven by money but by the lack. It works through lack and fictions thereof. If there is no lack, it invents it in order to go on. The thymotic economy describes human beings as creatures who want to give instead of take. Thymotic economies understand the human as someone with a deep propensity to give; this

is something one can observe in children, who are just as happy giving presents as they are receiving them.[17]

The fact, though, is that the form of mass culture which we practise today destroys (as Sloterdijk wistfully observes) communal consciousness 'through vulgarisation and egoism propaganda on a daily basis. There's probably no way around this in consumer societies. Today, the individual is first and foremost a consumer, not a citizen.' The consumer, let me add, extracts and detracts from the 'commons', whereas the producer adds and contributes to them. The citizen, ideally, is engaged in society's preoccupation with coordinating/balancing the taking with the giving, and keeping the 'commons' capable of securing both; with restoring cooperation between the two, disrupted by the rise of the 'erotic' over the 'thymotic' and the subsequent transformation of the human being 'into a zoon eroticon'.[18] Sloterdijk quotes from Simon Schama's *The Embarrassment of Riches*, representing the Netherlands as 'the first country in the world without a properly poor population. What did they do? The preachers ascended the pulpit and tried to frighten the rich by telling them that a wealthy life as such is a road to perdition.'[19]

Education, Literature, Sociology

Riccardo Mazzeo Having reached the last chapter of this second conversation, all the ideas I had thrown together in my mind in order to write something with a hint of meaning had become frozen, almost atrophied. Dissipated, dispersed, wiped out. I had never suffered from 'blank page syndrome', from that white page that cripples and every now and then embroils whoever sits down to write his personal thoughts. After all, I had never concluded a *second* work with my favourite friend/scholar/intellectual, and, as the Germans say, 'Einmal ist keinmal': no action, however commendable, has any value if performed only once.

In the correspondence between Paul Auster and J. M. Coetzee published in the volume *Here and Now*, at a certain point, after watching the DVD by Philippe Petit which shows a video interview made by his friend with a tightrope-walker, Coetzee voices his reservations on both the film and the tightrope-walker, and imagines a story better than the one told by Petit, 'a story that might have been outlined by Kafka and then discarded',[1] in which the tightrope-walker risks his life venturing out on a rope suspended in the void – he survives but resists trying the challenge again. He will get married, will have children but he won't be the same. Once is not enough.

I thought I would lose my sanity because I kept switching on the computer and then switching it off again without writing a single word. And I finally understood I needed to create a void, to get rid of all the hypotheses I had considered, ranging from thoughts taken from *The Possibility of an Island* by Houellebecq, a work so familiar to me that I asked all my friends to read it, to 'Pierre Menard, Author of the *Quixote*', mentioned in the book *Labyrinths* by Borges that you gave me when I last came to see you in Leeds – a work that is quite beyond my (although not superficial) comprehension right now, and that I feel unable to examine in any depth at this time.

Meanwhile, while travelling to Pordenone to meet my friend Massimo Recalcati, I read his latest book *L'ora di lezione*[2] on the train, and in it I discovered both the corroboration of my block and a possible means of escape from it:

> As Jung would say, every blank page carries with it the 'weight of yesterday', an invisible stratification of past memories that can imprison, subjugate, paralyze [. . .] Invisible yet dense accumulated knowledge settles on the blank white page covering it with a thick cobweb. [. . .] The white page is *always* filled with dead objects, inert elements, monumental ideals, and unattainable works because each creative process inherits all the memory of what has happened before. Nevertheless, this heritage has two possible destinies: either it can be compromised in the

form of scholastic repetition, or it can beget an authentically creative act.[3]

His book talks about the difficult art of transmitting knowledge that can become concretized only through the transmission of the *love of knowledge*. In my opinion, love of knowledge needs a fertile territory, rich in books and free from bureaucratic pedantry; open to participation from above and below, from near and far, resistant to that Mafia that emerges in the most exclusive schools. In these schools, the main purpose is not to expand knowledge and general well-being, but to create alliances with the children of those in power, who will one day take their parents' place. This is the way to perpetuate the privileged social class that permits the haves to control, together with their partners, the network whereby money produces more money and the destiny of the less fortunate is sold out.

I was reminded of the lesson given by Alan Bennett to certain Cambridge University students when the playwright recalled the matinees at the Grand Theatre in Leeds, his discovery of Cambridge in 1951 ('I had never been before in a place where beauty constantly continued to bloom'), his failure to be admitted to the university as a result of being too low down the social ladder, and the problem of independent education, which, as you wrote in our *On Education* (2012), neglects so many 'rough diamonds' and, as he underlined:

> if it is unfair then it is not even Christian. I do not know to what degree we owe to Christianity our ideas of justice. After all, souls are the same in the eyes of the Lord and are therefore worthy of equal opportunities, as they

say nowadays. This is certainly not the case in the field of education, and has never been, but it does not mean that we should give up trying. Is it not the time for a serious attempt?[4]

I reflected on what you said in the second chapter about the too few 'Lorenzinos' who can be saved by particularly good and generous teachers like Eraldo Affinati, who dedicates his life to those pupils who are by now considered as 'lost' – and also on the need for political solutions. Certainly, I do not see any strong signs that inspire hope on the political level. Coetzee recalls the hypothesis formulated by Borges of:

> an encyclopaedia that, once complete, would have the potential to replace the old past with a new past and therefore with a new present. [. . .] If applied to the financial crisis, Borges' proposal seems feasible, at least in theory. Compared to the history of mankind, numbers on a computer screen do not carry a lot of weight – not to the point that, if we wanted to, we could not come to an agreement and do without them in order to start over with a new set of numbers.[5]

Naturally, everything depends on us and our capacity to come to an agreement, but perhaps, as you wrote in your conversation with Gustavo Dessal, we need to wait for 'the return of the pendulum'.

Returning to the close link between sociology and literature, the problem that remains is that of opening up to horizons that are wider than our own circle and this is shared by both disciplines – as Auster writes to Coetzee: 'Nobody believes that poetry (or art) can change the world. Nobody is dedicated to a sacred mission. Today there are poets everywhere, but they only talk to each other.'[6]

Charles Wright Mills, to whom you paid homage, foresaw this closure in sociology. Like you, Wright Mills incarnates the figure of the 'maestro' described by Massimo Recalcati: able to trigger enthusiasm and throw open the doors of imagination. In his *The Sociological Imagination*, Wright Mills writes ironically to creatively describe and destroy the two prevailing theories of his time, the 'Grand Theory' by Talcott Parsons and the 'Abstracted Empiricism' of Paul Lazarsfeld. In the first case, he does this by quoting complex and incomprehensible pages by the author, then summarizing them in a few lines; in the second, he encourages the reader to carry out an experiment by describing a social context in its entirety while limiting this to the listing of statistical data on a small provincial town, without including all the information that is truly necessary for the task – forgetting, as stated by Benedetto Vecchi, 'history, social and "racial" stratification, migration flow, and the role played by religion, and political and federal administration'.[7]

Knowing that people are not computers, Wright Mills does not upload files of information into the brain of the reader: he does not want to teach by filling voids; on the contrary, he wants to open up new worlds to be explored and to do this he has to light a spark. I found the appendix to Wright Mills' book, 'On Intellectual Craftsmanship', wonderful and moving: there he explains how personal experience is 'so important as a source of original intellectual work' and tells his hypothetical student, 'By keeping an adequate file and thus developing self-reflective habits, you learn how to keep your inner world awake.'[8] Sociologists never want to develop passive reception in students (whether this involves the teachings of Schumpeter, Marx or Weber), but are always, and in every case, striving to stimulate re-processing and re-creation in order to attain 'three types of statement: *(a)* from some, you learn directly by restating systematically what the man says on given points as a whole; *(b)* some you accept or refute, giving reasons and arguments; *(c)* others you use as a source of suggestions for your own elaborations and projects'.[9]

Our students fool themselves that they can find 'all the answers' on the Internet, but a process of this kind is sterile, since: 'Just as it is foolish to design a field study if the answer can be found in a library, it is foolish to think you have exhausted the books before you have translated them into appropriate empirical studies, which merely means into questions of fact'.[10] And the sociologist explains the importance of moving from one perspective to another to become social science *scholars* – not simply technicians, trained to carry out predetermined processes. To tear away the curtain of pre-interpretation and to pronounce an original concept, it is essential to be able to pay attention 'to what is bound to be at first loose and even sloppy. But you must cling to such vague images and notions, if they are yours, and you must work them out. For it is in such forms that original ideas, if any, almost always first appear.'[11]

This is an attestation that is just as valid today as when Wright Mills wrote it, just before he died. On the other hand, imagination expressed in literature sometimes has similar value – for example, we need only to think of the last two novels by the Israeli author David

Grossman. Both works are influenced by the difficulty in bringing an end to the Israeli–Palestinian conflict and the death of his son Uri, killed in Lebanon in 2006. In the first, *To the End of the Land* (2003), a mother foresees that she could receive the news of the death of her son away on a military offensive. She decides to distance herself from the devastating revelation by going away on a hiking trip with two people dear to her in a zone where she cannot be contacted.

In the second, *Falling Out of Time* (2014), a man who has lost his son, once again through war, suddenly decides to leave his home and go 'there', to find the point of intersection between life and death. He begins to walk in circles around his town and gradually he is joined by others who have also lost children. With desperation, and at the same time with irony, the author tries to brush with death with the words he writes.

Recently, Grossman asked himself: 'How is it possible to protect the fragile bubble of a family in the midst of a war? In such an inhuman situation? Raising your children who must go and fight when they are 18?' And he added: 'In our country we tend to avoid reality, this vicious circle of violence, and we all do this, both Israelis and Palestinians. I have been opposing occupation for 30 years. As long as the Palestinians do not have their own state, we will not have a state either.'[12] In my opinion, this is a declaration that is perfectly valid, but infinitely less powerful than his wonderful books: imagination, analysis, imagination in analysis – this is the common destiny of sociology and literature.

Zygmunt Bauman   Auster's issue of whether arts can change the world applies in equal measure to sociology.

At the end of my overly long life, that question – together with the steadily rising volume of evidence to the contrary – is what worries me most. Looking back, what I see first, at the first glance, looks like a long series of false dawns and a vast graveyard of still-born hopes and aborted promises and expectations; of words discredited, discarded and forgotten well before they had a chance to become flesh.

And yet, called, as sociologists or novel-writers are, to help our fellow humans to see through their condition down to its most inner and arcane springs that derive their awesome power from their invisibility – to steer clear of its recondite traps and ambushes while searching for the ways to find or insert meaning, purpose and value in the way they live their lives – we have no other tools at our disposal but words. As the great José Saramago noted on 25 September 2008:

> right at the very beginning, before we invented speech, which is, as we know, the supreme creator of uncertainties [that is, in our dim animal past – ZB], we were not troubled by any serious doubts about who we were or about our personal and collective relationship with the place where we found ourselves [. . .] In its earlier phase, the world was nothing but appearances and nothing but surface [. . .] All things were just what they seemed.[13]

It is words that allow, prompt and oblige us to set apart what is from what seems to be; it is words that created the gap between the truth of the matter and its appearances, juxtaposing themselves against the suggestions/implications/insinuations of senses while attempting to articulate their messages and claiming the presiding chair in the tribunal of Truth. Nevertheless, the same Saramago, a mere two months later, on 18 November 2008, noted: 'I'm left with a bitter taste in my mouth due to the certainty that the handful of sensible things I've said in my life turned out after all to be of absolutely no consequence'; and he expressed that self-condemnation even if, undoubtedly, he had much less ground than most of us do to pronounce such a damning verdict on the practical effect of his life-long word-processing labour. Well, Saramago, one of the greatest philosophers and sociologists among novel-writers, set the standards for measuring the words' significance much higher than most of us dare and care to do; a month later, on Christmas Day, he wrote down: 'God is the silence of the universe, and man is the cry that gives meaning to that silence.'

Taking a leaf from one of the last interviews given by Cornelius Castoriadis, I noted, fifteen years ago, that 'the trouble with our civilization is that it stopped questioning itself'.[14] I also suggested that the proclamation of the downfall and demise of 'grand narratives' announces the disengagement of the knowledge classes: the grand refusal of the modern intellectual vocation, or what John Kenneth Galbraith memorably dubbed 'secession of the contented'. I also suggested that 'ideology used to set reason *against nature*; the neo-liberal discourse disempowers reason through *naturalizing* it'.[15] Being 'natural' means: having neither reason nor purpose. Just being. Ascribing 'naturalness' to a human-made, contrived and contingent sector/aspect of the universe is a cover-up operation for the self-complacent and self-congratulatory mood of a society that by and large (and starting from the top) has abandoned its ambition to set apart the *comme il faut* from the *comme il ne faut pas*, to fight back and conquer its avoidable ills, to correct the escapable errors of its ways, and, all in all, to assume responsibility (i.e., accept that 'it could have been done differently') for its choices – an unsavoury, and in the longer run toxic, mixture of smug self-approbation with craven self-deception.

The quandary of our time boils down to the neglect, refusal or learned incapacity of questioning. It is the art of articulating questions that wilts and fades, having fallen into disuse and been cast into disrepute by the hegemonic creed of TINA – 'There Is No Alternative' – as it was compactly and cleverly summarized in its time by Margaret Thatcher. As Michael Haneke, the director of films considered by their admirers to be 'fascinatingly disturbing', has formulated the purpose of his creative work: 'What is sought after is not ideology, but quarrelling with one's own lie.'[16] We may add that, whereas answers are invented, composed and offered for the sake of mitigating (and, better still, dispersing or stifling) anxiety and thereby putting quarrels to rest, the *raison d'être* of questions is to force the addressee out of a state of indifference and into a combative mood. Questions awake the questioned person to her or his obligation to choose and to carry responsibility for choosing and its consequences; in other words, they awaken the people whom they question to the moral nature of the self. Weiskopf prefers to classify Haneke's works as ethical rather than moralizing, belonging to the toolbox of Foucault's 'ethical psychagogy' rather than 'moral pedagogy': 'They dispense with persuasion, instruction or indoctrination and content themselves with confronting the spectator with a "truth" that demands a reaction or response and forces him/her to reflect on his/her self-relations.'

Let me add that such a truth is set against the pre-judgements of common sense, in as far as the truths promoted in psychagogy and in common sense are, as much as questions and answers, at cross-purposes. Questions tend to undermine the self-same mental and moral comfort that answers aim at founding. Wanting to arouse a 'productive restlessness in the viewer', Haneke – as Weiskopf rightly points out – 'not only seeks to make pain and suffering visible, but also to confront the spectator with his/her own ways of perceiving (or not perceiving) violence'. He documents this opinion by quoting Haneke's own view of the pernicious and dismal way in which violence is 'sold' and capitalized on in commercial films calculated for high box-office returns:

> Bad conscience doesn't sell. We all sit in the helicopter of *Apocalypse Now* and are firing the guns at the ant-like Vietnamese to the 'Ride of the Valkyries'; firing at what is alien, unfathomable, fear-inspiring, to be extinguished, and we feel as relaxed as having visited a sauna, because we do not have any responsibility for the massacre, because what is responsible for this is communism, the impenetrable political sleaze in Washington, or if needs be the American president, who isn't even a good friend of us. We all gladly pay seven euros for that, don't we?

Oh yes, we do! We pay for a clear conscience, as did our ancestors purchasing the indulgences for past and future sins marketed by itinerant monks. Such indulgences are nowadays a staple product of the commercialized culture industry in cahoots with the apostles of the status quo, notoriously preoccupied with fitting endemically rebellious moral selves into the immoral world, in order to disable the moral scruples that threaten to recut that world to the measure of the ethical demands they preach. The task of finding out what the possible/likely denouement of such a pre-designed or self-unravelling plot might look like, in case things and our way of setting them in motion are left on their present course, was left by Michel Houellebecq to Daniel 25, the last in the long row of cloned heroes in his masterpiece *The Possibility of an Island*: 'The joys of humans remain unknowable to us [neohumans]; inversely, we cannot be torn apart by their sorrows. Our nights are no longer shaken by terrors or ecstasy. We live, however; we go through life, without joy and without misery.'

Is this what we want? A happiness derived from the comforts of tranquillity, insensitivity and indifference? To Daniel 25, who got there with neither the right nor the capability to get out, it would not occur to describe his condition using the 'happiness' word.

The arrival of our era of lives consumed by consumerism – by a culture that views and treats the world as a huge, infinite and endlessly replenishable container of goods to be purchased, ingested, destroyed in the process of devouring or stripped of their lustre in the process of enjoying, and then disposed of on the waste tip – was prophetically foretold by another exceptionally talented and insightful novel-writer, Georges Perec, in the already quoted story of Sylvie and Jérôme, who discovered the delight of things that make life smooth, thorn-free, convenient and comfortable, and resolved to get rich in order to obtain such things galore.

In the world that was theirs it was almost a regulation always to wish for more than you could have. It was not they that decreed it; it was a social law, a fact of life, which advertising in general, magazines, window displays, the street scene and even, in a certain sense, all those productions which in common parlance constitute cultural life, expressed most authentically.[17]

Having explored a few tempting yet disappointing opportunities, they finally reached their goal. They were admitted to a 'strange and shimmering world, the bedazzling universe of a market culture, in prisons of plenty, in the bewitching traps of comfort and happiness'.[18] In such a world, their lives promised to be – they dreamt them to be – 'but the harmonious sequence of their days and nights, the one almost imperceptibly modulating the other, a never ending reprise of the same themes, a continuous happiness, a perpetuated enjoyment which no upset, no tragic event, no twist or turn of fate would ever bring into question'.[19]

There was a snag, though – and a thorny and vexing snag in that world of 'continuous happiness'. Time and again, our young couple 'could not stand it a moment longer. They wanted to fight, and to win. But how could they fight? Whom would they fight? What should they fight?'[20] Perec reminds us that in the past, much as in the present, millions of people fought, and go on fighting, for a morsel of bread and a glass of clean drinking water – but 'Jérôme and Sylvie did not quite believe you could go into battle for a chesterfield settee.' Who would? I can't abstain from recalling Wolfgang Goethe's idea of happiness, implied by his alleged response to the question whether, retrospectively, he considered his life to have been happy: 'I had a very happy life; though I can't recall a happy week.' Meaning: happiness does not derive from the absence of trouble, grief and distress, but from resisting, fighting and overcoming them.

Two years after *Les choses*, Perec published *Un homme qui dort*,[21] a philosophical contemplation of the certain end to the consumerist era that was just starting: 'Perhaps for a long time yet you could continue to lie to yourself, deadening your senses, sinking deeper and deeper into the mire. But the game is over, the great orgy, the spurious exaltation of a life in limbo. The world has not stirred and you have not changed. Indifference has not made you any different.' Regarding life's happiness-generating potential, there is a difference – a fully and truly immeasurable and interminable difference – between desiring to change the wallpaper and a desire to change the world and the plight of its residents.

Wallpaper and furniture, alongside the view from your window, your spouses and lovers, as well as your thoughts and yourself, are among the objects of consumption with which – as Joseph Brodsky, another visionary writer, predicts – you are bound to become bored.[22] Following insistent recommendations by the authors of advertising copies promising to insert a measure of excitement into the otherwise tediously unadventurous and monotonous succession of days and nights, you may try packing up all those used-up tokens of past enjoyment onto the nearest dumping ground – and probe the yet unexplored relishes of what looks like a 'new beginning' (i.e., new wallpaper, new window views, new lovers, etc.). If you think, though, that replacing the wallpaper or any other accoutrements of the consuming life will make for life's happiness, you are in for bitter frustration. As Brodsky warns – and as you, for the sake of the happiness you pursue (and on this occasion, also for the sake of a world somewhat more auspicious to human happiness), should read, ponder, memorize, take to heart – that phantom-like and hopelessly fissiparous happiness will last until the day (and not a day longer) 'when you wake up in your bedroom amid a new family and a different wallpaper, in a different state and climate, with a heap of bills from your travel agent and your shrink, yet with the same stale feeling toward the light of the day pouring through your window [. . .] Neurosis and depression will enter your lexicon: pills, your medical cabinet.'

These are fundamental existential issues, all but dissolved to the point of downright invisibility by the daily chase after new sensations and new beginnings – the trademarks of our hurried life, lived under the tyranny of the moment[23] in our intrinsically, and perhaps incurably, myopic society of consumers. They yearn to be restored to the centre of human attention, lest the modern dream of human autonomy, self-creation and self-assertion be cast beyond the limits of human capability.

Asking these and other fundamental existential questions, and bringing them back to the public agenda, are the vocations shared by literature and sociology. Pursuit of these questions unites the two creative pursuits – renders them complementary and sentenced to perpetual interaction and mutual inspiration.

Notes

Preface

1 Zygmunt Bauman, Michael Hviid Jacobsen and Keith Tester, *What Use Is Sociology? Conversations with Michael Hviid Jacobsen and Keith Tester* (Polity, 2014), pp. 14–17.

2 See Frederick Barth, *Ethnic Groups and Boundaries: The Social Organization of Culture Difference* (Universitetsforlaget, 1969).

3 On the pedigree and current phase of the 'two [opposite] cultures in one' issue, read Stefan Collini's highly informative and insightful article 'Leavis v. Snow: The "two cultures" bust-up 50 years on', published in the *Guardian* on 16 August 2013.

4 Here quoted from Georg Lukács, *The Theory of the Novel*, trans. Anna Bostook (The Merlin Press, 1971), pp. 72–3, 77.

5 Milan Kundera, *L'art du roman* (Gallimard, 1968); here quoted from *The Art of the Novel*, trans. Linda Asher (Faber & Faber, 2005), pp. 4–5.

6 José Saramago, *The Notebook*, trans. Amanda Hopkinson and Daniel Hahn (Verso, 2010), p. 13.

Chapter 1 The Two Sisters

1 Milan Kundera, *Le rideau: essai en sept parties* (Gallimard, 2005), p. 104.

2 Jean-Pierre Richard, *Proust et le monde sensible* (Editions du Seuil, 1974), p. 31.

3 Zygmunt Bauman, Michael Hviid Jacobsen and Keith Tester, *What Use Is Sociology? Conversations with Michael Hviid Jacobsen and Keith Tester* (Polity, 2014), p. 19.

4 Stefano Tani, *Lo schermo, l'Alzheimer, lo zombie: tre metafore del ventunesimo secolo* (Ombre corte, 2014), and Adolfo Fattori, *Sparire a se stessi: interrogazioni sull'identità contemporanea* (Ipermedium Libri, 2013).

5 Bauman et al., *What Use Is Sociology?*

6 Mario Luzi, *Al fuoco della controversia* (Garzanti, 1978), p. 43.

7 J. M. Coetzee, *Diary of a Bad Year* (Harvill Secker – imprint of Random House, 2007); *Diario di un anno difficile* (Einaudi, 2008), p. 121.

8 In Italian, *Il libro del riso e dell'oblio* (Adelphi, 1991).

9 Ibid., p. 217.

10 David Lodge, *Deaf Sentence* (Penguin Books, 2009), p. 32.

11 Milan Kundera, *Une rencontre* (Folio, 2011).

12 See www.opendemocracy.net/5050/heather-mcrobie/what-should-we-do-about-radovan-karadzic-poetry?

13 See www.smh.com.au/action/printArticle?id=277 4200.

14 Ibid.

15 Susan Sontag, 'Fascinating Fascism', a review of *The Last of the Nuba* by Leni Riefenstahl and *SS Regalia* by Jack Pia, *New York Review of Books*, 8 February 1975.

Chapter 2 Salvation through Literature

1 Eraldo Affinati, *Elogio del ripetente* (Mondadori, 2013).

2 Zygmunt Bauman, *Collateral Damage: Social Inequalities in a Global Age* (Polity, 2011).

3 Ibid., p. 1.

4 Ibid., p. 2.

5 Ibid., p. 3.

6 Richard Sennett, *Together: The Rituals, Pleasures and Politics of Cooperation* (Yale University Press, 2012).

7 Bauman, *Collateral Damage*, p. 9.

8 Affinati, *Elogio del ripetente*, pp. 12–13.

9 Ibid., p. 25.

10 Ibid., p. 50.

11 Paolo Rodari, 'A Villa Miseria dove abitano gli amici del Papa', *La Repubblica*, 2 March 2014, p. 32.

12 See Martha Nussbaum and Amartya Sen, *The Quality of Life* (Oxford University Press, 1993).

13 www.social-europe.eu/2011/08/the-london-riots-on-consumerism-coming-home-to-roost.

Chapter 3 The Pendulum and Calvino's Empty Centre

1 Zygmunt Bauman, Michael Hviid Jacobsen and Keith Tester, *What Use Is Sociology? Conversations*

with Michael Hviid Jacobsen and Keith Tester (Polity, 2014).

2 Zygmunt Bauman and Keith Tester, *Conversations with Zygmunt Bauman* (Polity in association with Blackwell Publishers, 2001).

3 Dominique Schnapper, *L'esprit démocratique des lois* (Gallimard, Collection Nrf, 2014).

4 Moisés Naím, *The End of Power: From Boardrooms to Battlefields and Churches to States, Why Being In Charge Isn't What It Used to Be* (Basic Books, 2013).

5 Marco Belpoliti, 'Quel che resta del potere' ('What Remains of Power'), *L'Espresso*, 27 February 2014.

6 Zygmunt Bauman and Riccardo Mazzeo, *On Education* (Polity Press, 2012), ch. 19.

7 Bauman and Tester, *Conversations with Zygmunt Bauman*, p. 145.

8 With a subtitle *Time, Chaos, and the New Laws of Nature* (The Free Press, 1996).

9 Ibid., pp. 4, 7.

10 Ibid., p. 37.

11 In Zygmunt Bauman, *The Art of Life* (Polity, 2008).

12 See Arlie Russell Hochschild, *The Outsourced Self* (Metropolitan Books, 2012), p. 8.

13 Ibid., pp. 11, 12, 14.

Chapter 4 The Father Problem

1 Luigi Zoja, *Il gesto di Ettore* (Bollati Boringhieri, 2000).

2 Ibid., pp. 10–11.

3 Ibid., p. 11.

4 Ibid., p. 12.

5 Zygmunt Bauman, *A Natural History of Evil* (Indigo Press, 2012).

6 Zoja, *Il gesto di Ettore*, p. 15.

7 Ibid., p. 45.

8 Ibid., p. 51.

9 Zygmunt Bauman, *Legislators and Interpreters: On Modernity, Postmodernity, and Intellectuals* (Polity, 1987).

10 Zoja, *Il gesto di Ettore*, p. 180.

11 Ibid., p. 181.

12 Ibid., p. 266.

13 Ibid., p. 297.

14 www.brainyquote.com/quotes/quotes/b/blaisepasc 151958.

Chapter 5 Literature and the Interregnum

1 Adolfo Fattori, *Sparire a se stessi: interrogazioni sull'identità contemporanea* (Ipermedium Libri, 2013), p. 11.

2 See 'Walser's Voice', in Robert Walser, *The Walk* (Serpent Tail, 1992), pp. vii–ix.

3 Robert Walser, 'The Walk', in Walser, *Selected Stories* (Farrar, Strauss and Giroux, 1982), p. 86.

4 Ibid., p. 52.

5 Robert Walser, 'Kleist in Thun', in Walser, *Selected Stories*, pp. 19–20.

6 Franz Kafka, 'The Departure', trans. Tania Stern and James Stern in *The Collected Short Stories of Franz Kafka*, ed. Nahum N. Glatzer (Penguin, 1988), p. 449.

7 See Martin Esslin in *The Theatre of the Absurd* (Doubleday, 1961), p. 138.

8 See W. G. Sebald, 'Le promeneur solitaire', *New Yorker,* 7 February 2014.

Chapter 6 The Blog and the Disappearance of Mediators

1 Jonathan Franzen, *The Kraus Project: Essays by Karl Kraus Translated and Annotated by Jonathan Franzen* (London, 2013), p. 25 of the Italian edition. All subsequent page references to this title apply to the Italian edition.

2 Franzen, quoted from *Die Fackel*, p. 50.

3 Zygmunt Bauman, Michael Hviid Jacobsen and Keith Tester, *What Use Is Sociology? Conversations with Michael Hviid Jacobsen and Keith Tester* (Polity, 2014).

4 Eugenio Borgna, *La dignità ferita* (Feltrinelli, 2013) and *La fragilità che è in noi* (Einaudi, 2014).

5 Franzen, *The Kraus Project*, pp. 79–80.

6 Ibid., pp. 70–1.

7 Ibid., p. 161.

8 Ibid., pp. 197–8.

9 See Jonathan Franzen, *Farther Away* (Fourth Estate, 2012), pp. 148–50.

10 See ibid., pp. 5–6.

11 Ibid., p. 11.

Chapter 7 Are We All Becoming Autistic?

1 Jean-Michel Besnier, *L'Homme simplifié: la syndrome de la touche étoile* (Librairie Arthème Fayard, 2012).

2 Theodor Adorno, p. 38 in the Italian edition, *Minima moralia: meditazioni della vita offesa* (La Biblioteca di Repubblica-L'Espresso, 1979 and 1994).

3 Besnier, *L'Homme simplifié*, p. 22.
4 Ibid., p. 52.
5 Ibid., p. 28.
6 See www.autistica.org.uk/about_autism/index.php?
   gclid=CjoKEQjwxZieBRDegZuj9rzLt_ABEiQAS
   qRd-hfAx6DsonYMiMfV8ti83_5robAAVnpZOjo2
   BJ5PoZcaAt_a8P8HAQ.
7 See www.autism.org.uk/about-autism/autism-and-
   asperger-syndrome-an-introduction/what-is-autism.
   aspx.

Chapter 8 Metaphors of the Twenty-first Century

1 Zygmunt Bauman, Michael Hviid Jacobsen and
   Keith Tester, *What Use Is Sociology? Conversations
   with Michael Hviid Jacobsen and Keith Tester*
   (Polity, 2014), p. 84.
2 Ibid., p. 78.
3 Ibid., pp. 78–9.
4 Ibid., p. 77.
5 Ibid.
6 Stefano Tani, *Lo schermo, l'Alzheimer, lo zombie:
   tre metafore del XXI secolo* (Ombre corte, 2014).
7 Ibid., p. 9.
8 Ibid., p. 40.
9 Ibid., pp. 66–7.
10 Marshall   McLuhan,   *Understanding   Media:
   The Extensions of Man* (McGraw-Hill, 1964),
   p. 49.
11 Tani, *Lo schermo, l'Alzheimer, lo zombie*, p. 74.
12 Lisa Genova, *Still Alice* [2007] (Simon & Schuster,
   2009).
13 Ibid., p. 33.
14 Ibid., pp. 268, 269.

15 Zygmunt Bauman, *Homo consumens* (Erickson, 2007).

16 Tani, *Lo schermo, l'Alzheimer, lo zombie*, p. 91.

17 See http://hundredgoals.files.wordpress.com2008/07/17australia-pope-attacks-consumerism.

18 'In His New Series Jacques Peretti Shows How Determined People Are to Get Us Buying Stuff. And Just How Willing We Are to Comply', *The Guardian*, 28 June 2014.

19 Georges Perec, *La vie: mode d'emploi* (Hachette, 1978).

20 Georges Perec, *Les choses* (René Juilliard, 1965). Quoted below from David Bellos' translation *Things: A Story of the Sixties* (Vintage Books, 2011).

21 Perec, *Things*, p. 35.

22 Thornstein Veblen, *Theory of the Leisure Class* (1899).

23 Thornstein Veblen, *Conspicuous Consumption* (Penguin Books, 2005), pp. 57–8.

24 Nicolas Rousseau, 12 July 2014, www.actu-philo sophia.com/spip.php?article382.

25 See Christopher Lasch, *Culture of Narcissism: American Life in an Age of Diminishing Expectations* [1979] (W.W. Norton & Co., 1991), p. 50.

26 Ibid., pp. 50–1.

27 Ibid., pp. 27, 33, 64.

28 Ibid., p. 242.

29 Michael Maccoby, *The Gameman: The New Corporate Leaders* (Simon & Schuster, 1976), p. 104. Here quoted after Lasch, *Culture of Narcissism*, p. 44.

30 Lasch, *Culture of Narcissism*, p. 44.

31 Jean M. Twenge and W. Keith Campbell (eds.),

The Narcissism Epidemics: Living in the Age of Entitlement (Atria Paperback, 2013), p. 259.

32 Lasch, *Culture of Narcissism*, p. 248.

33 Ibid.

Chapter 9 Risking Twitterature

1 Dubravka Ugrečić, *Cultura Karaoke* (Nottetempo, 2014); original title *Karaoke Culture / Napad na minibar* (2011).

2 Ugrečić, *Cultura Karaoke*, p. 16.

3 Ibid., pp. 22–3.

4 Ibid., p. 56.

5 Corinne Atlas, 'Un problema con la letteratura', *Internazionale*, 22 August 2014, no. 1065, p. 80.

6 Ugrečić, *Cultura Karaoke*, p. 103.

7 Ibid., p. 58.

8 Ugrečić, *Cultura Karaoke*, p. 56.

9 I quote from the English edition, *Karaoke Culture*, trans. David Williams (Open Letter, 2011), p. 39.

10 Ibid., pp. 40–1.

11 Ugrečić, *Cultura Karaoke*, pp. 22–3.

12 Ugrečić, *Karaoke Culture*, p. 43.

13 Quoted after Thomas Y. Levin's translation *The Mass Ornament* (Harvard University Press, 1995), pp. 65, 71.

14 Siegfried Kracauer, in another essay, 'Die Wartenden' ('Those Who Wait'), *Frankfurter Zeitung*, 12 March 1922, pp. 132, 129–30, 130–1.

Chapter 10 Dry and Damp

1 Alberto Garlini, *La legge dell'odio* ('The Law of Hate') (Einaudi, 2012).

2 Charles Wright Mills, *The Sociological Imagination* (Oxford University Press, 1959, 2000), p. 8.

3 Garlini, *La legge dell'odio*, p. 548.

4 Ibid., pp. 590–1.

5 Ibid., pp. 71–2.

6 Ibid., p. 555.

7 Ibid., pp. 621–2.

8 In its American University of Minnesota Press edition of 1987 under the title *Male Fantasies*.

9 Jonathan Littell, *Le sec et l'humide* (Gallimard, 2008).

10 Ibid., p. 35.

Chapter 11 The Retrenchment Within 'Oneness'

1 Jonathan Littell, *Les bienveillantes* (Paris, 2006); Italian translation: *Le benevole* (Einaudi, 2007), p. 18; English translation: *The Kindly Ones* (Harper Collins, 2009). Subsequent page references from this title apply to the Italian edition.

2 Ibid., p. 24.

3 Ibid., p. 496.

4 Robert Musil, *Der Man ohne Eigenschaften* (Rowohlt Verlag, 1930); Italian translation: *L'uomo senza qualità* (Einaudi, 1958), p. 654; English translation: *The Man without Qualities* (Alfred A. Knopf, 1995).

5 Musil, *L'uomo senza qualità*, p. 668.

6 Ibid., p. 672.

7 Zygmunt Bauman and Gustavo Dessal, *El retorno del péndulo: sobre psicoanalisis y el futuro del mundo líquido* (Fondo de Cultura Económica de España, 2014).

8 Littell, *Le benevole*, p. 382.

9 Ibid., p. 383.
10 Ibid., p. 440.
11 Bauman and Dessal, *El retorno del péndulo*, p. 27.
12 Littell, *Le benevole*, p. 144.
13 See Richard Sennett, *Together: The Rituals, Pleasures and Politics of Cooperation* (Penguin, 2012), p. 19.
14 Joke Brouwer and Sjoerd van Tuinen (eds.), *Giving and Taking: Antidotes to a Culture of Greed* (V2_ Publishing, 2014), p. 5.
15 See Peter Sloterdijk, 'What Does a Human Have That He Can Give Away?', in Brouwer and van Tuinen (eds.), *Giving and Taking*, pp. 10–11.
16 See http://wordinfo.info/unit/3363/ip:5/il:T.
17 Sloterdijk, 'What Does a Human Have That He Can Give Away?', p. 17.
18 Ibid.
19 Ibid., p. 18.

Chapter 12 Education, Literature, Sociology

1 Paul Auster and J. M. Coetzee, *Here and Now: Letters (2008–2011)* (Vintage, 2013), p. 127.
2 Massimo Recalcati, *L'ora di lezione* (Einaudi, 2014).
3 Ibid., pp. 45–6.
4 *London Review of Books* (www.lrb.co.uk).
5 Auster and Coetzee, *Here and Now*, p. 129.
6 Ibid., p. 87.
7 Benedetto Vecchi, 'Un sapere ridotto in frammenti', *Il manifesto*, 4 September 2014.
8 Charles Wright Mills, *The Sociological Imagination* (Oxford University Press, 1959, 2000), p. 197.
9 Ibid., p. 202.
10 Ibid., p. 205.
11 Ibid., p. 212.

12 David Grossman speaking in Pordenonelegge, during his conference in September 2013.

13 José Saramago in *O Caderno*, here quoted from Amanda Hopkinson and Daniel Hahn's translation published by Verso in 2010 under the title *The Notebook*.

14 Zygmunt Bauman, *In Search of Politics* (Polity, 1999), p. 125.

15 Ibid., p. 128.

16 Michael Haneke, quoted after R. Weiskopf, 'Ethical-aesthetic Critique of Moral Organization: Inspirations from Michael Haneke's Cinematic Work', *Culture and Organization*, 20, March 2014, pp. 152–74.

17 See Georges Perec, *Les choses* (Julliard, 1965). Here quoted from *Things: A Story of the Sixties*, trans. David Bellos (Vintage Books, 2011), p. 49.

18 Perec, *Things*, p. 77.

19 Ibid.

20 Ibid.

21 Here quoted from *A Man Asleep*, trans. Andrew Leak, in *Things*.

22 See Joseph Brodsky, *On Grief and Reason: Essays of Joseph Brodsky* (Farrar, Straus and Giroux, 1995), pp. 107–8.

23 A phrase coined by Thomas Hylland Eriksen in a study under the same title (Pluto Press, 2001). For an extended discussion, see also Zygmunt Bauman, *Consuming Life* (Polity, 2007), ch. 3.